IDIOT-PROOFING
DEMOCRACY

Dr. Jennifer M. Booker

IDIOT-PROOFING DEMOCRACY

Reimagining
the U.S. Constitution

THE
UNBOUND
PRESS

Hey unbound one!

Welcome to this magical book brought to you by The Unbound Press.

At The Unbound Press we believe that when women write freely from the fullest expression of who they are, it can't help but activate a feeling of deep connection and transformation in others. When we come together, we become more and we're changing the world, one book at a time!

This book has been carefully crafted by both the author and publisher with the intention of inspiring you to move ever more deeply into who you truly are.

We hope that this book helps you to connect with your Unbound Self and that you feel called to pass it on to others who want to live a more fully expressed life.

With much love,

Nicola Humber

Founder of The Unbound Press

www.theunboundpress.com

This book is dedicated to Sophie Magdalena Scholl and the thirty million Allies and resistance fighters who died in World War II fighting against fascism. May such sacrifice never be needed again.

CONTENTS

FOREWORD   xv

INTRODUCTION   1
Sources of Inspiration   3
Bipartisan Foundation   3
The Middle Rules   6
Founding Fathers' Limitations   8
The Challenge of Complete Requirements   10

COMMON GROUND   13
Role of Government   13
Type of Government   14
Type of Economy   16
Voting Rights   17
Equality – Sex and Gender Identity   18
Equality – Gender Presentation   19
Equality – Racial   20
Equality – Religious or Lack Thereof   23
Equality – Personal Relationships   25
Equality – Housing   27

EXISTING STRUCTURAL FAILURES   29
Money Buys Congress   29
Clueless Leaders   31
Financial Conflicts of Interest   32
Free National Security Clearances   33
Lifetime Careers of "Public Service"   35
Number of Congresspeople   37
Eternal Territories   38
Sustainability   40
Bodily Autonomy   43
Define Personhood   46
Animal Personhood   46
Gerrymandering   47

Gun Laws   48
Supremacist Backlash   49

NEW CLAUSES   53
Ban Slavery and the Electoral College   53
Ban Capital Punishment   53
Fashion and the Law   54
Marital Status   55
Sex and Gender Identity   55
Sexual Preference   58
Technology Changes   58
Summary of Features   60

ABOUT THE UNIFIED STATES CONSTITUTION   63
REFERENCES   63

PREAMBLE   3
ARTICLE 0 – FOUNDING PRINCIPLES   4
Section 0.1 – Life   4
Section 0.2 – Fallibility   4
Section 0.3 – Personal Dignity and Actualization   5
Section 0.4 – Government Purpose   5
Section 0.5 – Legislative Purpose   5
Section 0.6 – Punishment Authority   5
Section 0.7 – Role in Nature   5

ARTICLE 1 – INTRODUCTION   6
Section 1.1 – Inspiration for this Constitution   6
Section 1.2 – Branches of Government   6
Section 1.3 – Type of Government   7
Section 1.4 – Type of Economy   7
Section 1.5 – International Relations Goals   7
Section 1.6 – Property Ownership   7
Section 1.7 – Duties of the People   8

ARTICLE 2 – EXECUTIVE BRANCH   9
Section 2.1 – Office of the President   9

2.1.1 – Define President's Cabinet 9

2.1.2 – President Qualifications 9

2.1.3 – President Election and Term of Office 9

2.1.4 – Removal of President 10

2.1.5 – President Responsibilities and Powers 10

Section 2.2 – Office of the Vice President 11

2.2.1 – Vice President Qualifications 11

2.2.2 – Vice President Election and Term of Office 11

2.2.3 – Removal of Vice President 12

2.2.4 – Vice President Responsibilities and Powers 12

Section 2.3 – Office of the Armed Forces 12

2.3.1 – Define Military Master 13

2.3.2 – Armed Forces Departments 13

2.3.3 – Define Department Secretaries 13

2.3.4 – Required Military Service 13

2.3.5 – Veterans' Affairs 14

Section 2.4 – Line of Succession 14

ARTICLE 3 – LEGISLATIVE BRANCH 15

Section 3.1 – The House of Representatives 15

3.1.1 – House Purpose 15

3.1.2 – Electoral Districts Scope 16

3.1.3 – Electoral District Boundaries Defined 16

3.1.4 – Representative Qualifications 16

3.1.5 – Representative Term 17

3.1.6 – House Chief Representative Defined 17

Section 3.2 – The Senate 17

3.2.1 – Senate Purpose 17

3.2.2 – Number of Senators 17

3.2.3 – Senator Qualifications 18

3.2.4 – Senator Term 18

3.2.5 – Chief Senator Defined 18

Section 3.3 – Congress Impeachment 18

ARTICLE 4 – JUDICIAL BRANCH 20

Section 4.1 – National Supreme Court 20

4.1.1 – National Supreme Court Justice Qualifications 20

4.1.2 – National Supreme Court Justice Term   21
4.1.3 – National Supreme Court Justice Selection   21
Section 4.2 – State Supreme Courts   21
4.2.1 – State Supreme Court Justice Qualifications   21
4.2.2 – State Supreme Court Justice Term   21
4.2.3 – State Supreme Court Justice Selection   22
Section 4.3 – Core Legal Principles   22
4.3.1 – Rule of Law   22
4.3.2 – Personhood   22
4.3.3 – Voting Rights   23
4.3.4 – Immunity from Prosecution   23
4.3.5 – Martial Law   23
4.3.6 – Treason Defined   23
4.3.7 – Air and Sea Boundaries   24
4.3.8 – Single State   24
Section 4.4 – Pretrial Rights   24
4.4.1 – No Arbitrary Arrest or Custody   24
4.4.2 – Presumption of Innocence   24
4.4.3 – No Self Incrimination   24
4.4.4 – Right to Representation   25
4.4.5 – Proportional Bail   25
Section 4.5 – Trial Rights   25
4.5.1 – Right to Trial   25
4.5.2 – No Double Jeopardy   25
4.5.3 – Judicial Decisions   26
4.5.4 – Speedy Trial   26
4.5.5 – Right to Appeal   26
Section 4.6 – Punishment Rights   27
4.6.1 – No Collective or Kin Punishment   27
4.6.2 – No Capital Punishment or Torture   27
Section 4.7 – Recusal of Justices   28
Section 4.8 – Impeachment of Justices   28

ARTICLE 5 – BILL OF RIGHTS   29
Section 5.1 – Personal Rights   29
5.1.1 – Equal Rights Statement   29
5.1.2 – Survival Rights   29

5.1.3 – Right to Healthcare   29
5.1.4 – Right to Bodily Autonomy   29
5.1.5 – Freedom from Religion   30
5.1.6 – Equal Protection   30
5.1.7 – Personal Movement   30
5.1.8 – Marriage   30
5.1.9 – Workers' Rights   30
5.1.10 – No Slavery   31
5.1.11 – Right to Heritage   31
5.1.12 – Consumer Protection   31
5.1.13 – Environmental Protection   32
5.1.14 – Parenthood Rights   32
5.1.15 – Children's Work Rights   32
Section 5.2 – Communication Rights   32
5.2.1 – Free Speech   32
5.2.2 – Freedom of Media   32
5.2.3 – Right to Assembly and Association   33
5.2.4 – Right to Petition   33
5.2.5 – Right to Personal Ideology   33
Section 5.3 – Property Rights   33
5.3.1 – Right to Bear Arms   33
5.3.2 – No Soldiers on Private Property   34
5.3.3 – Search and Seizure   34
5.3.4 - Eminent Domain   34

ARTICLE 6 – OTHER CONSIDERATIONS   35
Section 6.1 – Federal versus State Legal Scope   35
6.1.1 – Federal Law Scope   35
6.1.2 – States' Powers   35
Section 6.2 – Constitutional Amendments   35
Section 6.3 – Citizenship   36
6.3.1 – Automatic Citizenship   36
6.3.2 – Acquired Citizenship   36
6.3.3 – Right to Citizenship   36
Section 6.4 – Science and Education   36
6.4.1 – Science-Based Policies   36
6.4.2 – Measurement   37

6.4.3 – Education   38
Section 6.5 – Campaign Contributions   38
Section 6.6 – National Census   39
Section 6.7 – Candidate Fitness for Duty   39
  6.7.1 – Qualifying Exams   39
  6.7.2 – Health Assessments   39
  6.7.3 – Financial Assessments   40
  6.7.4 – Security Clearances   40
  6.7.5 – Applicability and Exemptions   41
Section 6.8 – Official Language   41
Section 6.9 – Taxation   42
Section 6.10 – Budgetary System   42
Section 6.11 – Territory Status   42
Section 6.12 – Definitions   42

REFERENCES   45
APPENDIX A. MAPPING TO SOURCE DOCUMENTS   47
APPENDIX B. THE UNITED NATIONS' UNIVERSAL DECLARATION
OF HUMAN RIGHTS   61
APPENDIX C. THE SEVEN FUNDAMENTAL TENETS OF THE
SATANIC TEMPLE   69
APPENDIX D. GREEN PARTY TEN KEY VALUES   71

ABOUT THE AUTHOR   75

FOREWORD

It's no secret how dysfunctional the United States government has become. Unlimited greed, brittle egos, and partisan justices have warped interpretation of the Constitution into something that would have made the Founding Fathers blanche, while the intended safeguards (checks and balances) have been deliberately ignored.

The author's approach says the existing system is too broken to fix piecemeal, so her solution is to keep key concepts from the Constitution and start over. Rewrite and restructure the Constitution. There are many special interest organizations:

> End Citizens United (corporate personhood). Protect women's healthcare rights. The Equal Rights Amendment. Separation of church and state. LGBT rights. Protect the right to bear arms. End the Electoral College. Marriage rights. Universal healthcare. Workers' rights to unionize. Fight voter suppression. Racial inequality and the death penalty. And many more.

What if WE FIX THEM ALL AT ONCE? That's the goal here.

Keep the three-Branch structure (Executive, Legislative, and Judicial). Add term limits to keep people from becoming entrenched in government. Force people to prove they are minimally qualified to serve in the position to which they have been elected or nominated, which the author calls Fitness for Duty assessments. Clarify critical human rights and legal principles such as Separation of Church and State, and Innocent until Proven Guilty. Look for inspiration from recent outstanding Constitutions such as Norway and the Ukraine as well as ancient foundations such as the Magna Carta and the Iroquois Nations.

The target audiences for this book include: 1) anyone interested in understanding and improving the American government, 2) people outside the United States wondering how we went off the rails, 3) fledgling countries looking for democracy best practices, and 4) students of political science who want to learn from a proudly left-wing utopian view of government.

INTRODUCTION

This document explains the motivation behind major United States Constitutional changes needed to implement a sustainable democracy. This document is motivated by critical omissions from the United States of America Constitution and intends to prevent debates about "what the Founding Fathers intended." **While written primarily to improve the US Constitution and government, such as through a massive Constitutional Amendment, it could also be used as a foundation for a new State (country).** Accordingly, this is written from the perspective of the United States of America, but other views are included for perspective and balance.

A new Constitution is needed because the omissions and cultural legacy aspects of the United States' Constitution are too extensive to be addressed piecemeal. We have limited documentation on the cultural norms and assumptions from the 18th century, and yet it appears that they were influential in writing the Declaration of Independence and the Constitution for the United States of America.

Critical assumptions about fundamental human rights, legal principles, and the role of the country in the world need to

be stated explicitly to prevent corruption by antidemocratic forces.

To reflect these substantial changes, notice that the name of the State is changed to the **Unified** States of America, not the **United** States of America. In political science lingo, a State is a country, not a subdivision of a country such as a province, administrative region, or administrative division. [REF039] The Founding Fathers of the United States recognized this distinction. **Here the author will use "State" to refer to an entire country, and "state" to refer to a unit within a State, such as Minnesota or California or Bavaria.**

During the American Civil War, individual states who had seceded each issued their own currency. The author had paper money from Tennessee, South Carolina, and other Confederate states. A United State issues currency only at the Federal level. The term Unified is used here to mean that the individual states agree on basic government structure and human rights but retain their unique character within the larger State. If you think that human rights are wrong or negotiable, you're missing the point about them being "rights."

As a child, the author found it amusing that theoretically a person could be elected to office in the United States whose stated goal was to be a dictator. She never expected it to occur in her lifetime or ever.

The title of this book, *Idiot-Proofing Democracy*, is stated with the knowledge that idiots and fools are ingenious, so it is impossible to make something truly idiot-proof. It's like the problem faced by park rangers to design a garbage dumpster that is bear-proof but still usable by tourists. "There is considerable overlap between the intelligence of the smartest bears and the dumbest tourists." [REF112]

Any democratic system of government can be subverted if the people who are supposed to provide checks and balances on each other deliberately fail to do so. That's why this book is titled *Idiot-ProofING* not *Idiot-Proof*. The most we can hope for is to make it more difficult to corrupt.

Sources of Inspiration

The United States' Constitution was based on several previous documents, including the Articles of Confederation, Magna Carta, [REF075] the Charters of the Virginia Company of London, the Virginia Declaration of Rights, and the Declaration of Independence. [REF044]

This document draws from the United Nations' 1948 Universal Declaration of Human Rights, [REF119] the Constitution of the United States of America, [REF013] the Seven Tenets of the Satanic Temple, [REF068] Norway's Constitution of 1814 with Amendments through 2014, [REF085] the Green Party Ten Key Values, [REF094] the Constitution of Ukraine, [REF045] the Magna Carta, and the Iroquois Constitution. [REF089] **The author's intent is to blend her ideas with the best and most relevant elements from these sources.** This is intended to be an "industry best practices" version of a democratic Constitution, though to be fair, the Norway and Ukraine examples are already excellent.

The draft *Constitution for the Unified States of America* which follows maps its sections to those sources in Appendix A.

The author also draws from her earlier writing about political topics such as gun control, [REF059] sex chromosomes, [REF062] an early draft of this Constitution, [REF061] and many other topics. [REF060]

Bipartisan Foundation

Recall that political views are generally divided into left and right wings, where *the left wing is characterized by an emphasis on* "*ideas such as freedom, equality, fraternity, rights, progress, reform and internationalism*" *while the right wing is characterized by an emphasis on "notions such as authority, hierarchy, order, duty, tradition, reaction and nationalism."* [REF031] The left wing is associated with anarchists, communists, socialists, and Democrats. The right wing is associated with monarchists, fascists, and Republicans.

Historically, American Democrats and Republicans have both been to the right of the political spectrum and have even switched places with each other occasionally. Democrats used to be more right-wing, and Republicans used to be more left-wing. President Lincoln was a Republican, and signed the Emancipation Declaration, freeing the slaves. President Ronald Reagan was a Republican with very consistent views throughout his life but in 2025 would be dismissed by MAGA (Make America Great Again) Republicans as horribly progressive.

Calls for a third party have noted for over a century that Democrats and Republicans are "the left wing and the right wing of the same bird of prey." [REF001] The last significant showing by a third-party candidate was Ross Perot in 1992. He ran as an Independent, and got nearly 20 million votes, but zero electoral college votes. [REF020] Bill Clinton won that election by a large electoral college margin, 370-168 over George H.W. Bush but by fewer than six million votes. The electoral college is a vestige left over from slavery, to give slave states more power in presidential elections without recognizing slaves as human beings. [REF117]

Attempts to introduce more moderate or "progressive" views are blasted with scare tactics of being "radical" and "extreme" and so on. Even "liberal" is used as an insult, so Democrats are now labeled "progressive" instead. However, compared to international political standards, "radicals" like Senator Bernie Sanders are barely in the middle of the left-right "political compass" spectrum (Figure 1).

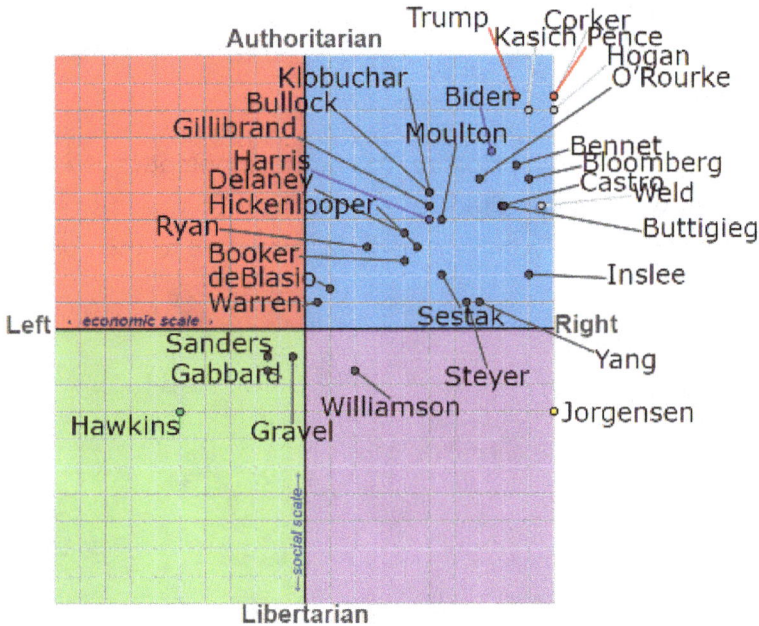

Figure 1. Political Compass for USA candidates during 2024
[REF056]

In the context of the political compass, Left and Right are economic views, with Left favoring taxes on the wealthy, more business regulation, and taxes used for social infrastructure. The Right favors low taxes, deregulation, and smaller government. Libertarian government favors personal freedom and equality, whereas Authoritarians favor compliance with government control.

Notice that Kamala Harris, Joseph Biden, and Donald Trump are shown in order of increasing authoritarian and right-wing beliefs. It is unclear why Tulsi Gabbard is shown in the lower left quadrant because she has been far further right wing than that as of this writing in early 2025. Perhaps her views are very fluid. As recently as 2020, she was a Democratic candidate for President. We have seen many politicians who adopt a false party label in order to get votes, such as Manchin, Sinema, and Case. The Booker shown in Figure 1 refers to Senator Cory Booker (D-NJ), no relation to the author.

In the interest of full disclosure, the author's perspective is in the extreme lower left quadrant of the political compass spectrum. Figure 2 shows how common party labels relate to the compass.

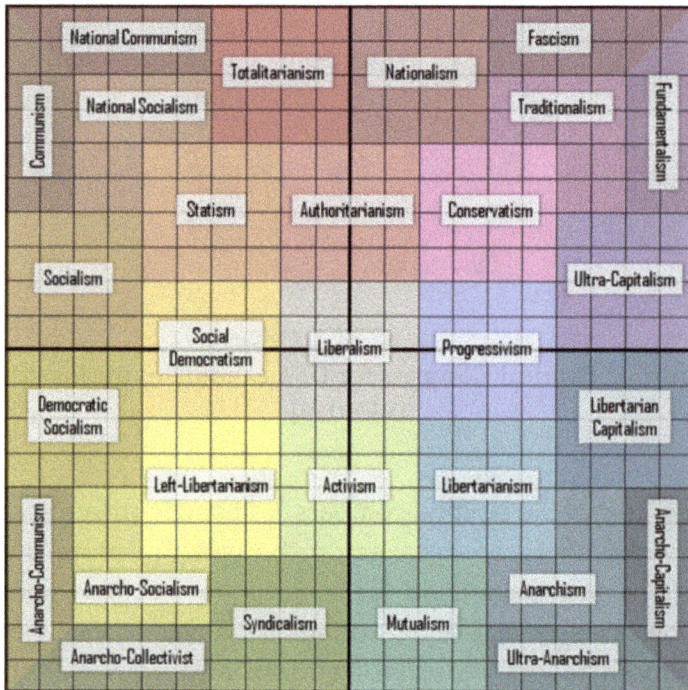

Figure 2. Political Labels and the Political Compass [REF064]

The Middle Rules

A key problem with the two-party system is that people on either extreme of the political spectrum (far left or far right) are not likely to change their position. A tree-hugging hippie from Northern California is not suddenly going to support massive corporate tax cuts and throwing away environmental regulations. A billionaire real estate developer is not going to push for higher income taxes.

As a result, presidential elections are largely decided by the "undecided" voters who live in the moderate or middle part of the spectrum. Third-party candidates tend to act as a spoiler for the major parties, drawing their votes from the left or right. This creates an environment that actively discourages the growth of third-party candidates.

For example, a frequent US Green Party presidential candidate is Jill Stein. The small number of votes she received in "swing" states (the states most evenly divided between the two major parties) were speculated to take votes from the Democratic candidate and led to a very slim margin of victory in those states for the Republican candidate in 2016. As a result, some Democrats attacked the Green Party for making them lose the election, even though both parties are nominally left-wing and have many similar views.

In the 2024 presidential election, the Independent candidacy of Robert F. Kennedy (RFK) Jr. was a confusing factor for both major parties, because the Kennedy family is legendary for being Democratic, but RFK Jr. is politically far from Democratic. In the end, RFK Jr. ended his bid and joined former President Trump's campaign.

Other countries can have several major political parties, and the one winning the most votes forms a "coalition" to blend their perspectives and get a majority of voters to support them. For example, the German Parliament (*Bundestag*) in 2025 elected 630 representatives, coming from five parties who earned 64 to 208 seats each. [REF048] The most extreme example the author is aware of is Italy, which can have hundreds of parties on the ballot. A famous example is Cicciolina (Ilona Anna Staller), an adult film star who was elected to the Italian Parliament in 1987 under a libertarian Radical Party. [REF028]

The two-party system in the United States has led to massive pandering to the people in the moderate or middle of the political spectrum, the last-minute "undecided" voters, and legislation crafted solely for the benefit of major corporations and special interest groups, who in turn openly support the candidate who helped them.

It is time to push for unapologetic support for human rights and a democratic government that tolerates capitalism but moderates unabashed greed.

That is the goal of these proposed Constitutional changes.

Founding Fathers' Limitations

The United States' government was based on a balance between liberal and conservative perspectives, between central Federal power and rights of the states. The law-making bodies House and Senate were based on favoring large population states and small population states, respectively. The Senate was modeled on being a board of directors for the country, to have a more long-term perspective and prevent radical shifts in government policy.

The body of the Constitution defined the major structures and responsibilities of the federal government, but the people insisted on adding the Bill of Rights (Amendments 1 to 10) to specify individual rights. To be fair, for writing in the 18th century, they did an excellent job.

Nevertheless, the technology of the 18th century was woefully unprepared for the future. Gun rights, for example, were based on muzzle-loading firearms with flintlock ignition. [REF033] An expert might be able to fire 2-3 rounds per minute, and rifled barrels had just been invented which might give a range of 300 yards, if rain didn't snuff the exposed flintlock gunpowder. The concept of a militia, often ignored by modern gun rights advocates, was a local group of men who were trained under a captain to help defend against Native Americans and other local armed forces, such as the French or Spanish. [REF077]

In contrast, modern firearms can readily fire hundreds of rounds per minute, and trained marksmen routinely hit targets at 1000-2000 yards. [REF109] Anything today calling itself a "militia" is most likely a right-wing paramilitary group. The closest today to the Revolutionary War-era militia would be the Army National Guard which has about 360,000 active members, just over 1/1000 of the population. [REF006]

As the author has summarized in a giant summary of world history events, [REF063] the vast majority of tools and technologies that we take for granted on a daily basis didn't exist before the middle of the 19th century. The Industrial Revolution led to increased wealth disparity. The oil, steel, railroad and newspaper industries became wealthy and powerful, such as the Rockefeller, Carnegie, Vanderbilt, and Hearst empires, respectively. They weren't shy about flaunting their wealth using real estate, such as the 135,280 square feet (sq ft) Biltmore Estate in North Carolina, and the 90,000 sq ft Hearst Castle in California. For comparison, a small single-family home might have 1000-1200 sq ft of living space, and a large one twice that.

It didn't take long for these empires to flex their proverbial muscles in the law. The Supreme Court bowed to their power in 1886 and decided that a corporation was a person in some respects. [REF066] This precedent has led to many controversial related rulings, discussed later.

In the late 19th century, many of the first cars were powered by electricity, and by the early 1900s, a third of cars were powered that way. But when Henry Ford started mass production of cars in the early 20th century, he pushed the electrical cars out of business by only mass-producing gas-powered cars. In the 21st century, we still see family empires pushing coal and petroleum use, even though both are non-renewable resources.

The Challenge of Complete Requirements

In many ways, writing a Constitution is trying to define the requirements for a government. The US Constitution originally only described the three Branches of government, but then the people said it needed to add the rights of individuals, which became the Bill of Rights, Amendments 1 to 10. Individual rights were a huge requirements omission.

In engineering terms, understanding and describing the requirements for a system, be it a car or computer application or government, is a critical step to ensure that the final product will serve its intended purpose. Many requirements describe what the thing can do, or what you can do with it, called *functional* requirements. "A car must have seating for five adults" could be a requirement for a sedan but wouldn't make sense for a convertible or a large SUV. Other requirements describe how well the thing does its job, such as *performance*. "A car needs to go from 0-60 mph in under 10 seconds" would be fine for a sedan, but sad for a sports car. Still other requirements describe *constraints* or limitations. "A car can't be more than 8 feet wide in the United States."

Likewise, a Constitution describes the structure of government, such as the three Branches, but also the activities or processes it must support, such as elections or impeachment, and define human rights, which are a kind of constraint on allowable activities or laws.

Why the digression about requirements? Because **the hardest requirements to define are often the ones that are the most obvious.** A story to illustrate this.

Once upon a time, the author was a young engineer for the Navy. Her facility had a large storage area behind the office space. An engineer, some 25 years her senior, wanted a vacuum cleaner to help tidy up the storage area. But to avoid bias or wasting money, he couldn't just go buy one and charge the government. He had to write requirements for a vacuum cleaner (!), submit them for competitive bid from at least three sources, and the lowest bid got this tiny contract. After months of going through this process, the vacuum cleaner finally showed up one day. Yay!!! The engineer went to use the hose attachment and found there wasn't one. It was a requirement so obvious that he never wrote it down.

There are several requirements for government that may have been too obvious for the Founding Fathers to address directly but are defined in this Constitution.

- What is the purpose of government?

- Who has the authority to punish people?

- What is the purpose of a legislature?

- What is the purpose of the judiciary?

- Define the principle of "separation of church and state."

- Define a person is "innocent until proven guilty."

- Define the "system of checks and balances."

- When is a child responsible for their actions? When are their parent(s) responsible?

- And the most contentious issues: When are you legally a person? When are you no longer a person?

COMMON GROUND

In order for a government to be sustainable and accepted by its citizens, the government must be based on common ground, i.e., principles that everyone can agree upon.

Role of Government

Government is a set of structures and rules to improve the safety and happiness of our citizens and residents and guide our interaction with other States.

The Preamble for the US Constitution [REF014] is a bit vague. In school, did you memorize "in Order to form a more perfect Union, establish Justice, insure domestic Tranquility, provide for the common defence, promote the general Welfare, and secure the Blessings of Liberty to ourselves and our Posterity, do ordain and establish this Constitution for the United States of America?"

A "more perfect Union" refers to bringing the states together into a single State. "Establish justice" is done by the judicial branch of government. "Insure domestic tranquility" is vague, the author assumes happiness covers it. The "common defense" is covered by safety. And finally, the "general Welfare" and "Blessings of Liberty" are also parts of happiness.

The Preamble didn't cover international relations, which is addressed here by "guide our interaction with other States." The world is a lot smaller in the 21st century, so that seems a bigger priority than the days of wooden sailing ships and horse-drawn carriages.

Type of Government

The Unified States of America are based on a representative democracy. That means that representatives are elected by the citizens. Given the large population of the State, a true or Direct Democracy is not feasible, because the citizens would all have to vote on every single bill proposed by the legislature (Congress). That would be pure chaos!

The single-person (dictatorship, monarchy) or single-party (totalitarian, authoritarian) types of government are not desirable, and most are what our European ancestors deliberately left behind in Europe. There is a famous photo from 1910 with nine European Kings who gathered at Windsor Castle for the funeral of England's King Edward VII (Figure 3). Many people would find it hard to believe that there were so many monarchs right before World War I, barely over a century ago.

Monarchs are sometimes given divine or infallible status, hinting at a theocracy (rule by divine guidance), but that brings a whole bunch of other problems. Monarchies are generally frowned upon now, and many have become constitutional monarchies to keep a limit on the monarch's power. Britain, Belgium, Cambodia, Jordan, the Netherlands, Norway, Spain, Sweden, and Thailand all have constitutional monarchies. [REF080] There are few true or Absolute Monarchies left today, including Brunei, Eswatini, Oman, Saudi Arabia, and Vatican City. [REF022] Those five absolute monarchies total about 42 million people, or only half a percent (0.5%) of the world population.

The author heard of an unconfirmed case years ago where a Saudi Prince got into a car accident and ran into a light pole. Being part

Figure 3. Nine Kings of Europe, 1910. [REF009]

Standing, L to R: King Haakon VII of Norway, Tsar Ferdinand of Bulgaria, King Manuel II of Portugal, Kaiser Wilhelm II of the German Empire, King George I of Greece, King Albert I of Belgium. Seated, L to R: King Alfonso XIII of Spain, King-Emperor George V of the United Kingdom, King Frederick VIII of Denmark

of the infallible royal family, the Prince legally could not have made a mistake, so the supervisor who installed the pole was demoted to punish him for installing it in the wrong place.

As a child, the author thought an oligarchy would be interesting, as in having five Presidents, for example. Given the challenges in electing one President, five would be impractical to say the least, and it would be far too easy for one strong personality to bully the others.

Some advocates of "small government" are using that to justify eliminating educational standards, environmental protections, international alliances, social healthcare, and many other government services. This seems to be headed toward a lack of government or anarchy. Some people seem to have an idealized view of anarchy, but examples such as Somalia show that weak federal government only produces conflict and chaos from regional leaders battling over power and resources.

There are many other types of government. [REF032] Some people suggest the United States is becoming a plutocracy (rule by the rich), kakistocracy (rule by the least competent), and/or kleptocracy (rule by theft). Time and perfect hindsight will tell. The term kakistocracy was first coined in a sermon in 1644 as a type of government even worse than anarchy. [REF106] There is a real government type called idiocracy, rule by the least competent, but the 2006 movie *Idiocracy* was about a very average person from the present seeming extremely intelligent far in the future. [REF099]

Type of Economy

The economy is "a system of production, resource allocation and distribution of goods and services within a society." [REF024] The distinction between a type of government and a type of economy is often confusing because some systems define both government and economy, such as anarchy, socialism, communism, feudalism, and many more.

The Unified States of America are based on a limited form of capitalist economy. A capitalist economy supports private ownership of property and the means of production (businesses, factories, farms, etc.), but State ownership of some types of production is needed to ensure that everyone benefits from critical resources.

Capitalism needs State intervention because capitalism has no moral center.

Pure capitalism is like the 1987 movie *Wall Street*, [REF097] in which the main character Gordon Gekko proudly states, "greed is good." Popular culture often glamorizes capitalism but ignores its heartless core.

Like millions of others, the author has fantasized about "what she would do if she won the lottery." Her fantasies are pretty specific up to winning about $100 million, but beyond that she has trouble imagining what else she'd do, other than more of the same. Yet there are at least 15 people in the world worth over $100 *billion*, and over 2700 "mere" billionaires. [REF041] The former have been dubbed *centibillionaires*, even though that is the wrong math prefix. The prefix centi- means 1/100th, but they mean hecto- which means 100x. [REF138]

A few billionaires have used their wealth for significant levels of philanthropy, such as Warren Buffet, Dolly Parton, and MacKenzie Scott, but most just sit on their dragon hoard and do everything possible to make it even bigger. **Capitalism encourages unlimited greed, so it is the responsibility of the State to temper that** by preventing the purchasing of government branches and ensuring fair income generation (taxes). That is a critical goal of *Idiot-Proofing Democracy.*

Voting Rights

"One person, one vote" applies to adult citizens of the Unified States of America.

"Adult" is defined as a person reaching the age of majority, typically 18 years, but also including minors who have declared emancipation from their parents. "Adult" excludes those who are not mentally competent, such as due to severe mental illness or catastrophic injury.

Voter suppression in the 2020s is often passed off as requiring expensive voter identification such as getting a passport or paying for a voter ID card. The alleged goal is to prevent fraudulent voting, which has been proven to be very rare. [REF144] Banning automatic registration to vote, voting by mail, or absentee ballots all suppress votes. [REF137] To protect against voter discrimination, **the Unified States bans charging directly or indirectly for registering to vote or voting.**

Convicted criminals will regain the right to vote after serving their sentence or after it was commuted (i.e., reduced or lessened by a Governor or the President). [REF130] If we are to expect ex-convicts to rejoin society, we must treat them as equals after they have paid for their crimes.

Equality – Sex and Gender Identity

Here is where it gets controversial.

There is no reason for government to judge a person based on their sex (male, female, intersex) or gender identity (masculine, feminine, gender queer, agender, etc.).

Many people with limited or incorrect education about biology attempt to impose binary sex labels (male or female) on people, but millennia of human history have shown that binary simply isn't true. Ancient cultures such as Egyptian or Sumerian recognized transgender people 3,000 to 4,000 years ago. Native American and other indigenous cultures around the world have honored "two spirit" or other gender non-conforming people for at least many centuries. [REF118] [REF134]

The author's sociology professor told class about being visited in India by a group of *hijra*, who insisted for several days on being given a small cash donation in return for blessing her newborn son. The *hijra* are a low social caste which includes a wide range of sex and gender identities as well as homosexuals. [REF026] Blessing newborn babies is their main source of meager income.

Equality – Gender Presentation

There is no reason for the government to judge a person based on their gender presentation (clothing, hairstyles, jewelry, fashion choices). Gender presentation is limited only by covering primary sexual and elimination organs in public.

Many European cultures have had a wide range of typical gender presentation over the centuries, but the last century has been focused on imposing Puritanical laws against cross-dressing, i.e., wearing clothes considered typical for the opposite sex. [REF027] As recently as 1923, it was illegal for women to wear pants in the United States, and many countries still have religion-based clothing prohibitions. [REF072] Many Native American tribes regard long hair for everyone as a sacred sign of strength, power, and a connection to nature.

Cultural norms for clothing and even clothing colors change. Around the year 1900, pink was seen as a better color for boys because it is a warm and hence more energetic color. Blue was for girls because it is a cooler, more passive color. [REF135] Dresses were worn by all babies because it was easier to change a diaper that way than wearing pants.

Anti-transgender laws since 2023 have focused on banning cross dressing in the form of drag shows. Meanwhile cartoons such as Bugs Bunny and pop culture stars starting with Charlie Chaplin have toyed with cross dressing for nearly a century (Figure 4) and no one was horrified. [REF023]

During the time of William Shakespeare (1564-1616), there were no actresses. Women's roles were always played by boys or young men. It was revolutionary to break that barrier in 1660. [REF136]

There is no basis for the government imposing arbitrary restrictions against people formerly known as transvestites. The Founding Fathers wore high heels, powdered wigs, and silk stockings, so

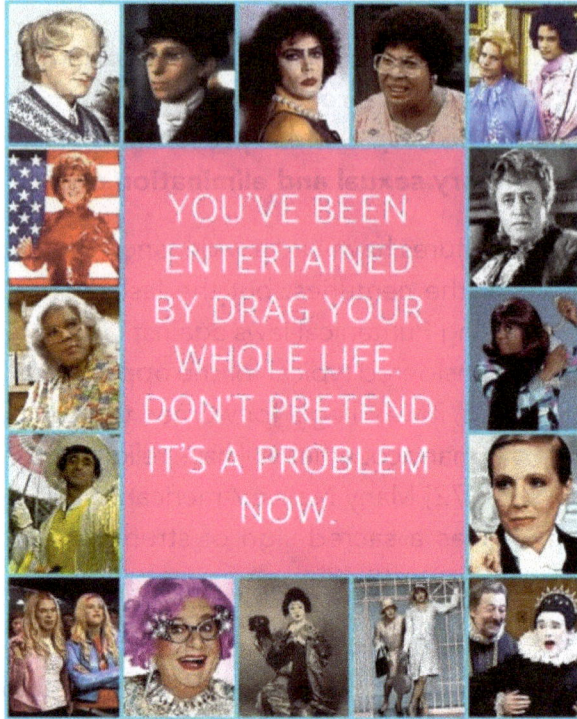

Figure 4. Cross Dressing Examples in Popular Culture

who are we to judge? **Doesn't the government have something better to do than be fashion show judges?**

For public health reasons, it is reasonable to cover external genitals and waste elimination organs (urethra, anus) at a minimum. Public bus seats can be scary enough as it is.

Equality – Racial

The Unified States ban any form of explicit or implicit discrimination based on racial or ethnic identity.

Race is an arbitrary cultural distinction, generally used as the basis for some imagined superiority. Scientists such as Johann Blumenbach and Carl Linnaeus tried to classify people according to skin color and skull characteristics, and early 20th century German scientists tried showing African natives had less brain volume. While Blumenbach tried to fit people into five races in 1825, even he admitted:

> All national differences in the form and colour of the human body [. . .] run so insensibly, by so many shades and transitions one into the other, that it is impossible to separate them by any but very arbitrary limits. [REF120]

These attempts at "scientific racism" were fully disproven by the middle 20th century. [REF037]

An embarrassing part of US history is that the modern American police forces were based on early 18th century Slave Patrols, whose purpose was to capture and return escaped slaves. Even after the 13th Amendment abolished slavery in 1865, the police were very active in enforcing Jim Crow laws. [REF050] The Jim Crow laws suppressed people of color through segregation until the mid-1960s. [REF030]

The justice system remains heavily biased against people of color through voter suppression, forced work for the incarcerated, mass incarceration, and a ban on citizen rights after serving a prison sentence. [REF124]

The author worked in a medium security prison as a nurse. The prisoners could get a job in the prison doing kitchen work, cleaning the facility, doing laundry, etc. They were paid 25 cents per hour (25¢/hr). Minimum wage was $14/hour.

In California, over 1,100 prisoners were put to work fighting massive wildfires in 2024, but as convicted criminals, after release they could not be hired as regular firefighters. Those prisoners were paid up to $27 per day to protect homes worth several million dollars each. [REF003]

As a child, the author recalls being told that there were four races – white (Caucasian), red (Native American, then called Indians), yellow (Asian), and black (African). With the advent of DNA studies, we have now shown that many European and Asian people have DNA from Neanderthals, and many people from Asia have DNA from a recently discovered (2010) prehuman species called Denisovans. The author's DNA analysis shows she has <2% of Neanderthal DNA, but still more than 64% of other 23andMe customers. *grunt, grunt*

[Language note for this book: "black" is used to describe people with more recent native African heritage because the author finds "African American" has nationality implications which are irrelevant.]

Israelis and Palestinians have fought over the Middle East desert for some 3000 years, but DNA shows that their ancestry is a lot more closely related than they would probably like to admit. [REF113]

The "Out of Africa Theory" is that all humans (*Homo sapiens sapiens*) are descended from Africa, starting with the first humans about 200,000 years ago, and from which people migrated starting about 100,000 years ago (Figure 5). Maternal DNA suggests there is a common female ancestor from East Africa about 150,000 years ago, nicknamed "Eve" because literally all modern humans are descended from her. [REF100]

Most Native American ancestors came across the Bering Strait bridge around 20,000 to 14,000 years ago, because the last Ice Age lowered sea level by 400 feet worldwide, making a literal land bridge between the continents. [REF065] There are other human migration theories, such as evidence from Australia that Aboriginal people have been there as long as 75,000 years. There are reports that some Central American native people may have come directly from Asia by sea, not via the Bering Strait. What cool stuff we have learned from DNA!

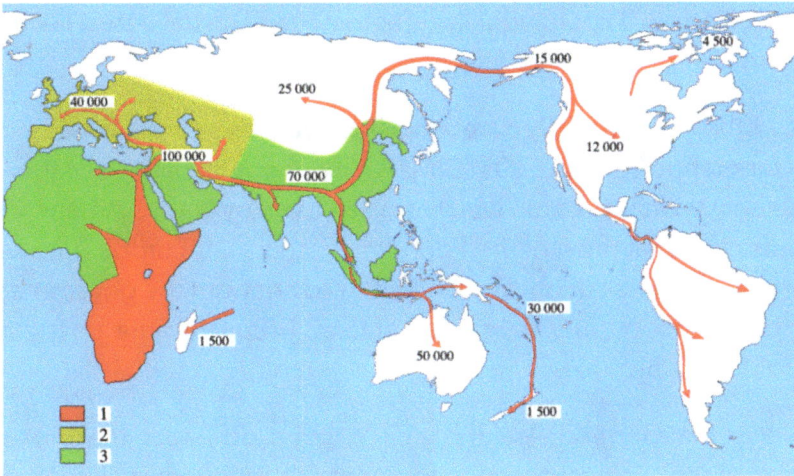

Figure 5. The Out of Africa Theory, showing how many years ago humans migrated from Africa. [REF008]

If humans all descended from African ancestors, and interbred with at least two types of pre-human species, it's absurd to claim that one "race" is superior. The author only recently learned that Caucasian was a derogatory term, used by white supremacists to claim a common heritage from the Caucasus Mountains in Eastern Europe. There's no proof of such a connection. They just made it up. The term Caucasian originated in the 1780s to describe white people, as opposed to black or Asian people. [REF129]

Equality – Religious or Lack Thereof

The Unified States will not discriminate on the basis of religion or lack thereof.

The United States required the motto "In God We Trust" on all currency in 1955, with some appearances of the phrase as far back as 1864. [REF029] Both of those time periods were a rise in religious fervor, and use of the phrase was defended by an appeals court as recently as 2018. [REF042] The phrase does not specify which God, so it could equally refer to Zeus, G-d, Ra, Jesus, Lucifer, or Brahma.

Nevertheless, the US Declaration of Independence and Constitution never mention God, Jesus, Christianity or any derivative of them. The only term is Creator, which is often used by Native Americans. It was clear that most of the Founding Fathers left Europe because of religious persecution, and explicitly did not want the government to be based on any religious sect. In 1786, Virginia passed a resolution which read:

> We the General Assembly of Virginia do enact that no man shall be compelled to frequent or support any religious worship, place, or ministry whatsoever, nor shall be enforced, restrained, molested, or burthened in his body or goods, nor shall otherwise suffer, on account of his religious opinions or belief; but that all men shall be free to profess, and by argument to maintain, their opinions in matters of religion, and that the same shall in no wise diminish, enlarge, or affect their civil capacities.

> —Virginia Statute for Religious Liberty, Section II. [REF010]

The phrase "or lack thereof" at the start of this section is a key feature, because nearly 30% of the population are atheist, humanist, agnostic, or otherwise have no religious affiliation. [REF110] They must have exactly the same rights as anyone else.

In addition, there is no reason to assume that all religions are "faith-based" because most pagan, tribal, or indigenous spiritualities are experiential or nature-based, not faith-based. Faith-based is sometimes used to indicate an inclusive religious view, but many faith-based religions are unaware of or dismiss the existence of nature religions.

Equality – Personal Relationships

The Unified States shall not discriminate on the basis of marital status.

The United States has made a very big deal out of marriage. A lot of it came from treating women as property. "You have to get married so your father can transfer ownership of you to your husband." Is that surprising to read? Why else would you "give away the bride" or expect women to take their husband's last name? "You have to be a virgin when you get married, or you aren't worth as much as a bride?" That statement only makes sense if a woman is a commodity to be purchased by her husband, and somehow a lack of previous intimate experience makes her more valuable.

Until 1974, women in the United States could not get a loan, credit card, or mortgage without a husband's co-signature. Those concepts of women and relationships are obsolete. The Equal Credit Opportunity Act finally gave women those rights. [REF069]

The author's paternal grandmother got divorced in the 1950s. It's hard to imagine how horrible her husband had to be to get a divorce in that era. Can you imagine getting a divorce when you have to fight for every basic right because you don't have a husband?

The author dated a lady who had recently left a 14-year committed relationship. They didn't get married because they were both young professionals, and their combined income would have greatly increased their income tax burden. They literally didn't get married for tax reasons.

A famous 2004 report by the US Government Accountability Office (GAO) identified 1,138 laws which are marriage-specific in the United States Code (Federal laws). [REF092] In many ways, marriage is legally a special type of business entity, which is reminiscent of its medieval origin as a way to secure business or political relationships between families or kingdoms (mocked in Figure 6). [REF105]

Figure 6. Medieval View of Marriage

Keeping the government out of the marriage business greatly simplifies a lot of laws. The IRS has been obsessed with your filing status as Married, Single, or Head of Household. What if all that didn't matter, and you just paid taxes based on your income and deductions?

There have been strong prohibitions in the United States against plural marriages, often called polygamy. The Mormon Church (a.k.a. Church of Jesus Christ of Latter-day Saints or LDS Church) in particular was a strong advocate for polygamy but changed their minds in 1904 after being threatened with federal prosecution. [REF035] Polygamy has often been very sexist, where a man can have multiple wives (called polygyny), but a woman can't have multiple husbands (polyandry). The author has known several successful expanded marriages such as "triads," which are three people in a committed relationship. Authors such as Robert Heinlein explored polygamy in some of their novels, such as *The Moon is a Harsh Mistress* (1966). [REF145]

Many people have mocked the Biblical argument claiming that "marriage is solely between one man and one woman." At least eight types of marriage have been based on Old Testament or Torah passages, [REF057] some involving slaves, concubines, prisoners of war, and other very non-nuclear family structures. King Solomon, circa 950 BCE, was said to have 700 royal wives and 300 concubines, and was only criticized because some of his wives worshipped foreign gods and not the Hebrew G-d. [REF038]

Regardless of people's choices for marriage or not, it really isn't the government's business. **There is no benefit to the public from the government micromanaging personal relationships among consenting adults.**

Equality – Housing

Home ownership has long been thought of as a safe investment toward retirement. It was encouraged after WWII to get women out of the factories and back in the home. Early planned single-family housing communities, such as Levittown just outside Philadelphia, PA, were inexpensive for first-time buyers, but then needed care for the home and maintenance of the lawn.

Home prices rise faster than inflation, so buying a home and keeping it at least five years will generally be profitable. The author's parents' first home in Nebraska was a large home on a corner lot and cost $18,000. Granted, at the time in the late 1960s, a salary of $10,000/year was considered very good. The author has owned two homes, and getting a mortgage typically requires your annual salary is at least 1/3 of the mortgage amount.

In the early 1990s, the author was a successful young engineer in Los Angeles, but the housing boom made it clear that she could never afford home ownership there. She was earning about $50,000 per year, but the cheapest livable homes started around $250,000. Saving 20% for a down payment ($50,000!) was hard to imagine, and even then, the payments would have been far more than she could have paid. A TV show gave an example of buying a $400,000 home in a nice neighborhood, and her eyes just rolled at the thought of an $80,000 down payment. Might as well have been a bajillion dollars.

In the United States, the interest on home mortgages is tax-deductible, which has the effect of encouraging home ownership. Actually all interest payments were deductible until 1986, when President Reagan got rid of the deduction for most kinds of interest. You could even deduct sales taxes if you kept detailed records of them. The origin of interest being tax deductible goes back to 1913, when it was justified because many people ran small businesses out of their homes, so trying to isolate business-specific interest was difficult. [REF058]

Even in 1913, Senator Sutherland realized that mortgage interest being deductible for individuals, but rent was not, was fundamentally unfair. The housing boom after WWII made it clear that home ownership was fueled by this deduction, but even in 2025, the unfair bias against renters still exists.

As a result, many people today are "rent poor," because they have to pay so much in rent that saving money to buy a home is nearly impossible. Their rent helps the landlord build equity, and the tenants have nothing to show for paying rent except they weren't homeless on the street.

The solution is to be consistent. Either make neither mortgage payments (and interest) nor rent deductible or make them both tax deductible. This isn't a huge philosophical issue for the Constitution, but it affects millions of people every day.

EXISTING STRUCTURAL FAILURES

This section focuses on ways in which the original intent of the US Constitution has been thwarted or corrupted since its inception. A critical assumption by the Founding Fathers was that the people elected or chosen for high level Executive, Legislative, or Judicial positions would be honorable men who were devoted to upholding the principles of the Constitution and their oaths of office. This assumption has been overcome by greed and lust for power, especially in the last few decades. **Greed is nothing new but has destroyed many cultures.**

Money Buys Congress

The United States of America tried to be an indirect democracy. Over time, its intent was subverted by a massive influx of special interest funds combined with legislators who made a life career of their positions, leading to an unstable and unfair plutocracy (government by the wealthy).

The richest American according to the Census in 1790, John Hancock, was worth the equivalent of under $10 million in today's money. [REF081] The levels of wealth hoarding seen today are wildly beyond anything the Founding Fathers could have imagined.

The number of registered lobbyists in Washington, DC is over 12,000, or about 23 lobbyists per member of Congress. They spent over $4 billion in 2022 wooing Congresspeople, so if you can't afford a flock of lobbyists, you have a hard time bending the ear of your representatives. [REF107]

For a long time, donations to political campaigns were strongly limited by law. There are still limits of $3,300 per candidate per year for an individual to contribute. [REF122] Limits on state races can range from a few hundred dollars per candidate to unlimited. [REF104]

Corporate donations were unleashed in 2010 with the *Citizens United* Supreme Court decision. [REF090] A corporation or special interest group forms a Political Action Committee (PAC), and the PAC can collect and distribute unlimited donations, provided they are not spent supporting a specific candidate. As a result of lobbying and donations, the people writing laws are flooded with huge contributions that will disappear if they don't support a certain special interest.

This has been described as the rise of "dark money" for campaigns, which can easily soar into billions of dollars. **Enormous and intended loopholes in *Citizens United* allow incessant attack ads on your opponent(s)** as long as you don't explicitly support your candidate. In addition to attacks on the other party's candidate, we have seen a lot of ads fueling distrust in government, raising doubt about the health of the economy, and other ways to create fear and distrust of the incumbents.

New members of Congress are advised that they are typically expected to spend several hours per day soliciting contributions from major donors. Not meeting with constituents, not writing bills, not meeting with colleagues to gain support for co-sponsored legislation, a huge part of their job is begging for money to fuel their campaigns.

How do we fix this? Keep it simple. **Ban corporate donations. Ban anonymous and PAC donations. Put a national and state cap on individual donations per candidate and per campaign. Ban lobbyist communication with candidates.**

Clueless Leaders

In recent years there has been an epidemic of people getting into high levels of Federal Service without an appropriate understanding of the role they are assuming. As people well beyond traditional retirement ages enter Service, frequent questions of physical and/or mental competence also arise. It is critical to keep people out of high offices just because they have good name recognition and/or wealthy supporters.

To prevent these issues, the Unified States shall assess **Fitness for Duty.** Upon first being elected or nominated for high-level Federal Service, **every candidate must pass objective tests of physical and mental condition called Health Assessments.** Physical and mental assessments need to be performed by providers who are fully qualified to do so and have no personal or financial connection to the people whom they are assessing.

Health Assessments are to ensure that candidates do not have chronic physical conditions and/or severe chronic mental illnesses that would prevent them from performing their duties. Health Assessments also verify that the candidate is not taking medications or supplements which could impair their judgment.

Candidates must also pass a written or oral test called **Qualifying Exams to demonstrate a fundamental understanding of Unified States history, government structure, checks and balances, basic economics, and international relations.** Such tests would have to be developed by nonpartisan scientists and validated to show objectivity. For example, basic history and citizenship knowledge could be adapted from a naturalized citizenship test.

Failure to pass after no more than two attempts will disqualify them from serving.

Financial Conflicts of Interest

Politicians have long had pressure to show that they do not have financial conflicts of interest while in office. President Jimmy Carter put his very modest Georgia peanut farm in a blind trust in 1977 after being elected. High-level members of the Executive, Legislative, and Judicial Branches of government have often provided several years of tax returns to show they do not have conflicting investments in foreign countries or major government contractors.

Sadly, there has been no enforcement of this, so recent massive and blatant conflicts of interest have not been removed, such as substantial foreign business activities and loan obligations, forcing government staff and foreign dignitaries to use politician-owned facilities, and paying huge cash amounts to meet with politicians. Cryptocurrencies such as Bitcoin have provided an untraceable way to funnel bribes to politicians.

Another obvious conflict comes with investments by legislators who know in advance when major government contracts are going to be awarded, and they can buy stocks in those companies before the announcement is made public. As noted in the movie *Wall Street*, this is called insider trading, and is wildly illegal for most people, but Congress often exempts themselves from legislation. [REF097]

The solution is simple. **Require financial disclosure before any high-level position in any Branch is filled.** No exceptions. No excuses. **Ban insider trading and exclusion of legislators from their own laws.**

Free National Security Clearances

Under normal circumstances, anyone who needs access to information which could threaten national security (such as military capabilities, intelligence resources, international relations strategies, classified information shared by allies, etc.) must qualify for a national security clearance on their own merits.

For even the lowest Confidential clearance, you have to prove you have no felony criminal convictions, no financial issues which would make you vulnerable to bribery, no connections or obligations to possible enemy States, and no close family members in enemy States which could be used to blackmail you (such as "give us X or we will kill your parents").

For many years, being a closeted homosexual was considered a red flag against having a security clearance, because you could be "outed" if you did not disclose classified information. This restriction on sexual preference was finally removed by Executive Order 12968 in 1995 because it had never been used to compromise classified information. [REF025] That Executive Order also added financial disclosure requirements for a security clearance to reveal vulnerability to bribery.

Unlike what you might see on TV or in a movie, real classified documents never just say CLASSIFIED, they are labeled with the highest level of security in the document, then every single paragraph, figure, and table is labeled with the security level of that item, such as [U], [C], or [TS]. That way, the reader knows exactly how classified every piece of information is.

The lowest security levels are Unclassified, Confidential, Secret, and Top Secret, but there are many levels of security above those, plus other qualifiers such as NOFORN (can't share it with non-American citizens), WNINTEL (Western Intelligence sources used to get it), OPSEC (operational security, such as current military action plans), RD (Restricted Data, reserved for nuclear weapon information), [REF087] and many more. Classified documents have cover sheets, as seen in Figure 7, to show the highest level of classification they contain. Cover sheets never have classified information on them.

Figure 7. Real cover sheets from classified documents.
[REF002]

A classification you might see on the *NCIS* TV show [REF098] is SCI, which is Sensitive Compartmented Information. Their video conference room, called MTAC, is presumably a SCIF or SCI Facility. A SCIF has been specially sealed to prevent any electromagnetic signals from leaving which could be intercepted and only uses highly encrypted computer connections. Intelligence and data encryption information are often TS/SCI, which is Top Secret and SCI.

You might hear reference to "black programs," which are so heavily classified that the real name of the program is itself classified. Black programs are given meaningless unclassified names, like Have Forum.

A massive exemption from sane legislation is that the President is immune to qualifying for a security clearance and can issue clearances for anyone he or she wants. Members of Congress also do not have to apply for clearances because they are assumed to be honorable people. Many recent members of Congress do not have any previous experience with national security information or military service and can easily let critical information slip.

In any other context, giving clearances without investigation would be unthinkable. **The solution is to require Executive and Legislative Branch members to qualify for security clearances like anyone else, with no exceptions.** That includes the President, Vice President, Cabinet, and all members of Congress. Judicial Branch justices do not need security clearances, because laws are never classified.

Failure to pass a security clearance investigation must disqualify a person from serving in that capacity.

Lifetime Careers of "Public Service"

When the Founding Fathers were drafting the Constitution, average life expectancy was about 35 years, due in large part to high infant and child mortality and dangerous work conditions. [REF101] People could live much longer – Benjamin Franklin lived to age 85 – but that was rare for people of more modest means.

Many of the Founding Fathers weren't yet old enough to be President (Monroe, Burr, Hamilton, Madison, and Jefferson) and only Adams and Washington were in their 40s. This is reflected in the Constitution, where the minimum ages for Congress and the Presidency are 30 and 35 years, respectively. They weren't expecting many people to live a lot longer.

Improvements in medical care have resulted in a much longer life expectancy today. Men in the USA expect to live about 73 years, women 79 years. [REF115] Nevertheless, life expectancy at birth for both sexes in the USA ranked 69th out of 183 countries studied by the World Health Organization (WHO) in 2019. [REF007]

Four Senators served from 47 to 51 years in office (Leahy, Thurmond, Inouye, and Byrd). President Joe Biden served 36 years in the Senate before being Vice President for eight years and President for four years. Four Representatives served from 48 to 59 years in office (Young, Conyers, Whitten, and Dingell). Representative Dingell was reelected 29 times by his Michigan district. [REF111] During the Cold War, the author's high school history teacher pointed out that members of Congress had a higher re-election rate than the Soviet Union's equivalent Politburo.

As a result of this trend, the average American is 20 years younger than their representatives in Congress. The average age of a Senator is 64, and the average Representative is 57 years old. [REF043]

It should come as no surprise that there is massive public support for term limits for Congress, but apparently no one in Congress is willing to do that to themselves.

The Justices of the Supreme Court have lifetime appointments, so partisan majorities in the Senate have taken to installing Justices who are much younger than the average. The four most recently added Justices are all in their 50s, and the rest range from 63 to 75 years old. [REF123] Term limits have been strongly suggested for the Justices, but no action has been taken.

Therefore, **it is proposed that term limits be applied to the President, Vice President, Congress, and the Supreme Court.** The President and Vice President can retain the current limit of two four-year terms. [REF012] Congress, both House and Senate, will have limits of 12 years – two six-year terms for Senators and four three-year terms for Representatives. Supreme Court Justices will serve a single term of twelve years.

The change in House term length is to give them more time to get something done. Under two-year terms, Representatives barely learn how their job works before campaigning for re-election. A three-year term should help give them more productive time. Three-year terms also deliberately stagger the election cycle so that odd-numbered years are important too and still prevent a sudden influx of extreme viewpoints.

A lifetime appointment for Justices of the Supreme Court brings in excessive influence on decisions from individual views and introduces many concerns about the onset of mental deterioration such as dementia. A single 12-year term will give them a good amount of continuity but prevent decades-long terms. William O. Douglas served on the Supreme Court over 36 years, ending in 1975. [REF116]

Number of Congresspeople

The size of each part of Congress was designed to favor large states (the House) and small states (the Senate). The point of this section is to meet two goals: 1) give a distribution of representation that is fair to both small and large states, and 2) give room for future growth so we don't need to fix this again later.

The number of Senators was defined by the United States' Constitution to be two per State. The number of Representatives initially increased with population but was fixed at 435 as a result of the 1929 Permanent Apportionment Act. [REF047] The country's population in 2024 is nearly triple (2.8 times) that of 1929.

When the first National Census was held in 1790, the least populous state was Delaware with about 59,000 people, and Virginia was largest with 692,000 people. Hence, the ratio of largest to smallest population was about 11.7 to 1. [REF125] In the 2020 Census, Wyoming had a population of 577,000, and California a population of 39,538,000. That gives a ratio of 68.5 to 1, over six times greater disparity than when the country was founded. [REF083] Today, a Senator from Wyoming represents 289,000 people, but a Senator from California represents 19,789,000 people.

On average, a Senator represents one percent of the population, or 3.3 million people. Based on this and to allow for future population growth, **assign one Senator per 4 million population, rounded up.** At present, this would give one Senator each for 24 States, and ten for California instead of two.

Given the total USA population of 331,449,000, each Representative represents an average of about 760,000 people. Each state has at least one Representative, so even Wyoming gets one. **Assign one Representative per 800,000 people** in an Electoral District, rounded up. Five states would get only one Representative who represents the single Electoral District. California would get 50 Representatives, only slightly different from its current 52 Representatives. [REF021]

Allow the number of Representatives and Senators to expand as the country grows. There is no benefit from expecting a single legislator to represent the will of tens of millions of people.

Eternal Territories

They are generally ignored by many people, but the United States has fourteen territories, three in the Caribbean Sea and eleven in the Pacific Ocean. Five of these fourteen territories are permanently occupied and have representation in Congress. [REF040] They are:

- American Samoa (became a territory in 1929), not the independent country of Samoa.

- Guam (1899)

- the Northern Mariana Islands (1986)

- Puerto Rico (1898)

- the U.S. Virgin Islands (1917), not the British Virgin Islands.

Saying the territories "have representation in Congress" is generous, since each has only one Representative in the House who is *not allowed to vote* on legislation, and zero Senators. The citizens of these territories cannot vote in federal elections but still have to pay income taxes. Recall that taxation without representation was a prominent factor leading to the Declaration of Independence. [REF139]

These five territories have a combined population of about 3.6 million people, with 95% of that in Puerto Rico. [REF034] The territories have a combined population greater than Utah or 20 other individual states, far more than could be reasonably dismissed. The last territories admitted to the United States were Alaska and Hawaii, both in 1959. Hawaii includes the mostly unpopulated Minor Outlying Islands, including the well-known Midway Island, some 1100 miles (1800 km) to the northwest of Kauai.

Most territories have been supporting the federal government for a century or more, and host critical military bases (even hear of World War II? Guam? Saipan? Tinian? Pago Pago?) yet are not given the same rights as other American citizens. Residents of American Samoa are not even granted US citizenship automatically.

There needs to be a time limit on status as a territory. Become independent, become a state, do something. To keep taking advantage of territories for decades on end is simply abusive, at the very least because of taxation without representation.

Sustainability

As a result of excessive influence by lobbyists and corporate donations, the focus of federal legislation has been severely short-sighted. The author believes that **a goal of government should be sustainability.** This should manifest in many areas such as not incurring excessive debt, long-term management of renewable resources, and avoiding long-term dependence on non-renewable resources.

The need for this change in perspective is to **counter the capitalist perspective of maximizing profit at any cost.** Under a purely capitalist economy, corporations will eagerly put children to work as soon as they can walk, destroy irreplaceable resources like old growth forests, push addiction to non-renewable fossil fuels, dump pollution anywhere until the lakes burn (a reference to the infamous Lake Erie fire in 1969), [REF011] and keep workers undereducated, underpaid, and overworked as much as possible.

Child labor was allowed until the Fair Labor Standards Act of 1938. [REF088] Before that, it was common to see children barely past toddler age working in fields, coal mines, sweatshops, and many other jobs. (Figure 8) By 1910, two million children from age 5 to 15 were employed in the United States, many in mines or other unsafe environments. [REF140] The popular musical *Newsies* was based on a strike by boys who sold newspapers on New York City streets in 1899. [REF131]

Mandatory education for children is a relatively new idea in the United States, though the rest of the world has seen it to varying degrees, such as Judaic culture ("rabbi" means "teacher"), the Reformation and Martin Luther in the 1520s, and Aztec culture also in the 16th century. Meanwhile in the USA, states initially defined mandatory education, ranging from Massachusetts in 1852 to the last, Mississippi, in 1917. [REF091] Individual states still define education laws, but the Federal Department of Education

Figure 8.1 A child cotton mill worker in 1820. [REF132]

Figure 8.2 Child coal mine workers in 1911 West Virginia [REF133]

provides guidance through the Elementary and Secondary Education Act of 1965. [REF093]

Another symptom of corporate shortsightedness is the emphasis on short-term profitability. Publicly traded corporations are generally run by a Board of Directors who can fire managers and even the CEO if they disapprove of the way the company is being run. Changes in stock price, amount and frequency of dividends paid, and other short-term measures are seen as critical, making a strong disincentive against long-term investments in infrastructure, basic research, employee satisfaction, and environmental protection.

Corporate power has also prevented investment in more sustainable technologies such as non-petroleum plastics and expanded use of hemp and bamboo products, which are much more efficient than wood-based paper and structural products.

Infrastructure has been a neglected topic for decades. As the country started using cars and trains more, President Roosevelt fueled massive spending on public infrastructure through the National Industrial Recovery Act (1933), better known as the Public Works Administration (PWA). [REF036] The next huge investment was under President Eisenhower in 1956, with the Federal-Aid Highway Act. [REF046] Decades passed with little support for infrastructure taken for granted by the public, until President Biden's Infrastructure Investment and Jobs Act of 2021. [REF084]

When fiscal support for fundamental infrastructure is at the mercy of public opinion polls and biased legislators, it is impossible for the country to be sustainable. People seem surprised when trains fall off their tracks or bridges fall into a river, but steel and concrete don't last forever.

In contrast, cultures around the world, many before written records were invented, knew of basic hygiene, water and sewer infrastructure, made artwork, and had structured societies. The Vikings, Aztecs, Mayans, Māori, people from Egypt, Turkey, China, Indonesia,

India, and our oldest ancestors from Africa all learned how to live in harmony with their environment for hundreds or thousands of years.

"Modern" civilization has destroyed most of the world's resources in less than 200 years. If we don't reverse this trend, there will be no one left to crew your megayacht or trim the bushes on your private island.

Bodily Autonomy

In 1973, the Supreme Court in *Roe v Wade* gave women the right to terminate a pregnancy before the fetus is viable outside the womb. In 2022, *Dobbs v. Jackson Women's Health Organization* took away that right at the federal level, stating that the constitutional right to "liberty" does not include the right to choose an abortion. [REF079] This ruling also may open the legal door to end same-sex and interracial marriage rights and other forms of privacy.

The Dobbs decision passed the right to determine bodily autonomy to the states to decide individually. This defies the concept of the states being unified under a federal government. It's one thing to say the states have some reserved rights, but another to allow wildly different interpretations of fundamental human rights to be decided by the whim of every state government.

It also discriminates against poor people to assume glibly they could just "go to a different state" if the healthcare they need is illegal in their state and possibly several neighboring states. Not everyone has a car. Not everyone can take days off work to travel for medical care. Not everyone can pay for gas and hotel bills to travel. Not everyone can afford to pay cash for an abortion or other basic medical care.

At its core, **the debate over abortion is one of bodily autonomy.** "Who has the right to decide what medical procedures I can have?" Most of the anti-choice arguments try to claim that the fetus is a person and therefore has protection. [REF055] Or it's phrased as determining when life starts. Some try to say it's at conception, which is impractical since no one knows they are pregnant immediately after conception. The *Roe v Wade* decision said it was at fetal viability: "When can a fetus survive if it is removed before full term?" The problem with that is that fetal viability has changed with advances in technology. It was widely assumed to be 24 weeks' gestation, but viability can be from 20 to 26 weeks. [REF071]

Another neglected issue is the cost of caring for extremely premature infants. Even if a NICU (Neonatal Intensive Care Unit) is available, it can cost $8,000 to $20,000 per day for basic care, not counting surgical or other procedures. Premature infants can have severe breathing issues because the lungs are among the last organs to develop, and the cost before they can leave the hospital can easily exceed one million dollars.

If a legislature wants to force women to give birth, who is going to pay for that care? Who is going to pay for drug rehab treatment for babies forced to be born to mothers with drug addiction? The author doesn't see "pro-life" activists lining up to adopt severely challenged newborn babies. Likewise, there is a dearth of legislation from pro-life activists for funding perinatal healthcare services, and most are eager to end funding for such services. Most "pro-life" focus seems to end at conception.

Some try to use Biblical justification, but separation of church and state rules that out. Besides, the Bible says a person has a soul when they first take a breath, as in the creation of Adam (Genesis 2:7). The Roman Catholic Church maintains the soul is created at conception. [REF103] These arguments can be decided after it is resolved how to measure a person's soul.

Others try to establish arbitrary deadlines for performing an abortion, such as six- or fifteen-weeks' gestation, which have no medical basis. Since gestation is measured from the start of the previous menstrual period, [REF121] and not at actual conception, which is rarely known, most people are not sure they are pregnant at six weeks' gestation, especially if they have an irregular menstrual cycle.

Attempts to ban abortion also ignore very important cases where an abortion is a medical necessity. The fetus can die from natural causes during pregnancy (*in utero*) and must be removed to prevent deadly infection (sepsis) for the mother. Ultrasound technology can also determine if the fetus is not going to be viable at any gestational age, such as when the fetus is severely deformed or missing vital organs.

The author assisted at third-trimester abortions (shortly after 24 weeks), and it's not something anyone would do unless absolutely necessary. Would you go through months of morning sickness, peeing every ten minutes, and becoming very visibly pregnant for six months or more only to "change your mind" on a whim? Some pro-life advocates even claim that abortions are done up to and even after birth, which is pure rubbish.

Legal restrictions on bodily autonomy also ignore a basic principle of healthcare. Healthcare decisions are made by people of sound mind, often in conjunction with licensed providers (MD, DO, DNP, PsyD, etc.). Nowhere does it state that uneducated and unlicensed politicians can decide which procedures are allowed. This means that **politicians are practicing medicine without a license by attempting to micromanage personal healthcare decisions.**

All of this assumes that the government can decide when a person gets a certain medical procedure. This violates laws of bodily autonomy that apply even after death. Anyone can decide if they want their organs donated after their death or even specify certain organs and not others. **To deny a person the right to a medical abortion or any other healthcare is to give them fewer rights alive than after they die.** That is no exaggeration.

Define Personhood

Related to bodily autonomy, it is important to define what a person is from a legal perspective. The simplest approach is to **define legal personhood as starting at the time of live birth.** Any time before that and you quickly devolve into discussions as futile as how many angels can dance on the head of a pin.

Rights pertaining to organ donation are clear that a person can define what happens to their body after death, therefore **legal personhood extends indefinitely after death.**

The absurdity of corporate personhood (e.g. Citizen's United) can easily be ended by declaring **personhood only applies to human beings.**

Animal Personhood

Some countries have started to define legal rights similar to humans for animals that exhibit advanced intellectual capabilities. For example, the Colorado Supreme Court had to address, "Do elephants, with their intelligence, sensitivity, friendships and capability, deserve personhood?" [REF086] [REF053] Similar questions have been raised for primates, whales, octopuses, and others. [REF054] [REF049]

While these questions raise massive legal, ethical, and logistical issues, and many people regard them as absurd, consider that business corporations have had some person rights in the United States for about 140 years. Nevertheless, **the question of animal personhood is beyond the scope of resolution here.**

Even though no one has given animals the rights of people, there have been formal legal and religious prosecutions of animals for centuries. [REF082] It's hard to imagine what people thought hanging a cat or pig would accomplish, but perhaps killing an animal for hurting a person is today's equivalent, just without the formal courtroom theater. If a lion gets loose and kills a person, the lion is just being a lion, a wild apex predator. End of story.

Gerrymandering

In the United States, after each ten-year census, the boundaries for Electoral Districts are redrawn in states that have more than one Representative. Electoral districts have been fine tuned into absurd shapes to select specific neighborhoods or even individual homes in order to control how many districts have a majority of voters for one party (Figure 9). Some degree of partisan bias is allowable under the Civil Rights Act of 1964, [REF114] but needs to be reigned in.

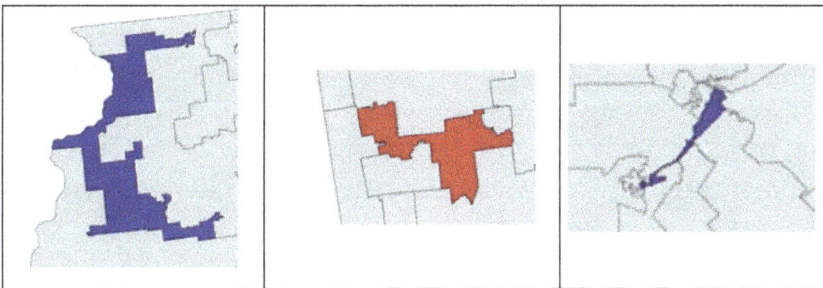

Figure 9. Examples of extreme gerrymandering in Illinois, Ohio, and Texas Electoral Districts. [REF067]

The author considered choosing Electoral Districts based on county boundaries, but many counties have far more people than would be feasible for one Electoral District. For example, the City of Los Angeles is also the County of Los Angeles and has a population of nearly ten million.

To resolve this, the author proposes a simple approach that would still give room for tweaking to give a slight partisan bias by the majority party but prevent gerrymandering. **Define an Electoral**

District using no more than six boundaries. A boundary is one of the following:

- The middle of a public roadway (street, road, avenue, etc.)

- The middle of a moving body of water (creek, stream, river)

- The coast of a stationary body of water (pond, lake, sea, gulf, ocean)

- A political boundary, such as the boundaries of a county, state, or the country.

This solution is elegant enough to be easily understood yet still provides the opportunity for a little wiggle room.

Gun Laws

Gun laws are a very sensitive topic, since American culture has glamorized firearms for centuries. The Old West, the rugged cowboy, the Lone Ranger, the renegade cop (Dirty Harry), the traumatized Vietnam veteran (John Rambo), all are lone men with guns who deliver some form of "justice."

Attempts to regulate firearms are fought feverishly by powerful lobbies [REF141] and legislators from states which have long traditions of firearms freedom. There are tens of thousands of firearms laws in the United States because they are state-specific and can have local ordinances as well. [REF108] Through the 1980s, it was common to see gun racks in the back window of pickup trucks. That's still often legal in many rural areas, but the gun can't be loaded, and theft is a big risk.

The 1934 National Firearms Act put a damper on fully automatic guns (fires more than one round per trigger pull, such as a machine gun), but a "bump stock" turns a semi-automatic gun (fires once per trigger pull) into effectively fully automatic without changing the trigger mechanism. Fully automatic guns are legal for the public, but only with a special permit and they had to be made before 1986. [REF146]

The rise of 3-D printers has made it possible to make a single-shot "ghost gun" at home with no traceability, [REF015] and guns can be made from ordering parts separately and assembling them yourself. Some older laws tried to define specific weight, caliber, and barrel length limits, but that doesn't accomplish much. All of this shows that **it is very difficult to write gun laws that will be effective but also tolerated.**

Supremacist Backlash

A driving force behind the political far right in the 2020s has been a backlash in response to more proof that white supremacy is a fiction. That's not to say there aren't a bunch of white men who are extremely smart and wonderful, the problem is that there are also a bunch of people of color and women who are also extremely smart and wonderful. Wouldn't it be great if we could benefit from both!? What a crazy liberal idea!

Much of the fuel for this backlash is the President Barack Obama administration (2009-2017). He embodies many of the things that white supremacists want to believe can't exist in a black man. He is very intelligent, handsome, well-educated, fit, articulate, and successful. He consistently ranks among the best presidents the United States has ever had.

The backlash produced support for Donald Trump, who has none of the traits of President Obama. He started his adult life with a $400 million gift from his father yet profited less from it than if he had just put it in a nice investment account. It takes special "talent" to bankrupt casinos, which are statistically guaranteed to be profitable, but he has. He refuses to allow anyone to see his alleged educational records, never exercises, eats only junk food, speaks in word salad, had at least six bankruptcies, and dozens of sexual assault allegations. In his first administration, he was impeached twice and convicted of 34 fraud felonies. He was found guilty of sexual abuse and defamation in 2022. [REF147] Several other state and federal prosecutions were put on indefinite hold because of his second term.

President Trump openly embraced white supremacists, mocked people with disabilities, and showed only contempt for anyone who wasn't white, wealthy, and of European descent. His appeal was to people with little or no education, terrible income, and deep resentment of people who remind them of how little they have. The states with the most support for Trump were also the ones with the highest rates of poverty, dependence on food stamps, teen pregnancy, and lowest rates of high school graduation. Trump relied on their rage to attack the political left instead of trying to provide more for his base.

Figures 10 and 11 show some of the people whom white supremacists probably resent.

In contrast, **the view of the Unified States is to raise everyone up instead of attacking those of whom we are jealous.** Provide a foundation of education and care to let ALL people find their strengths then explore and develop them.

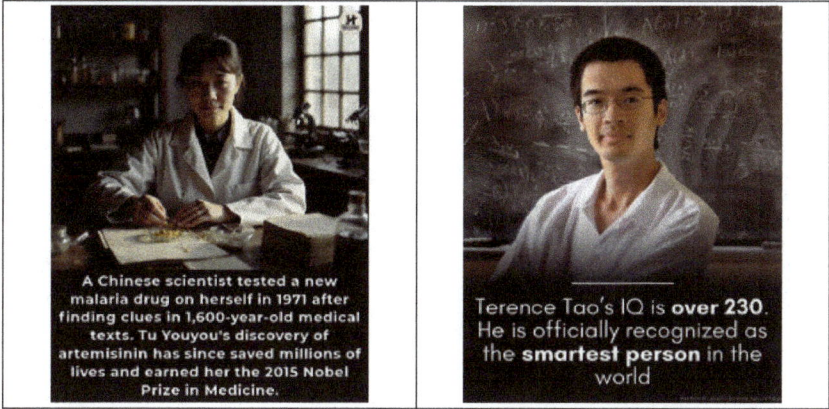

Figure 10. Modern Geniuses

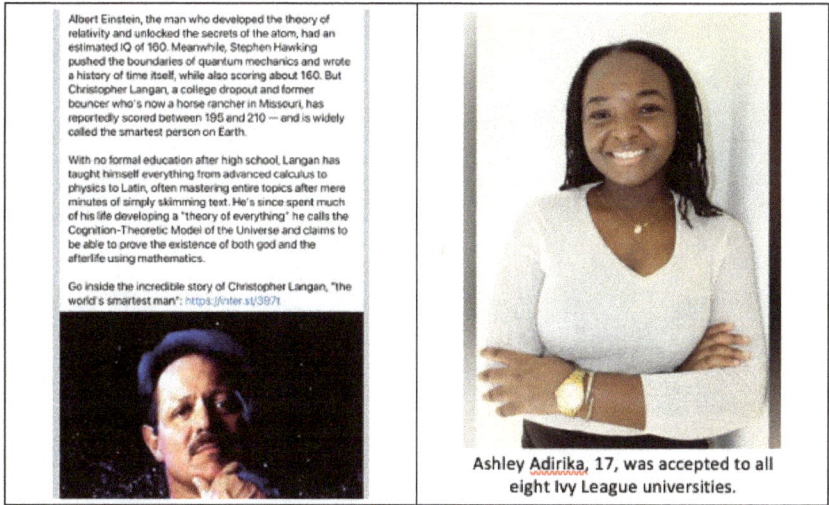

Figure 11. More Modern Geniuses

NEW CLAUSES

The Constitution needs new clauses to protect human rights and keep the government from meddling in frivolous topics.

Ban Slavery and the Electoral College

There is no need for the vestiges of slavery from the United States' Constitution, including the Three-Fifths Compromise, [REF052] which was abolished in 1868 by the 14th Amendment, [REF076] and the Electoral College. [REF074] Every presidential election, many Americans have clamored for the end of the Electoral College, but no one has proposed a Constitutional Amendment to make it happen.

Ban Capital Punishment

Capital punishment (the death penalty) has been used for at least 3,800 years, in the most draconian case for all crimes under the Draconian Code of Athens. [REF016] Yes, that's the basis for the adjective "draconian." The American Colonies practiced capital punishment as far back as 1608, and in the United States, the death penalty is still legal in 27 states. With all of this historical precedent, why ban it?

Over half of capital cases who were later exonerated were black people, [REF017] yet black people (African Americans) are only 13% percent of the population. There is massive racial bias in convicting black people of capital offenses. [REF018]

The death penalty is not a deterrent to murder. The National Research Council published a report in 2012 reaching that conclusion, *Deterrence and the Death Penalty*. The cost for prosecuting capital cases ranges from 3-8 times that of non-capital cases, so capital punishment is also far more expensive to prosecute. [REF019]

Capital punishment was justified partly under the biblical "eye for an eye" basis [REF078] but in practice has been used more as retribution instead of justice. If incarceration is inadequate to protect the public from rapists and murderers, then that is an issue for the correctional system to address, don't rely on capital punishment.

Therefore, **ban capital punishment. Ban torture as well.** The latter should be obvious, but the author overestimates the compassion of many people.

Fashion and the Law

Most laws regarding fashion have been to enforce strict gender-based clothing presentation. In the author's opinion, this is an utter waste of time for the government. It is absurd to see that women could be arrested 100 years ago for wearing pants. Women wear suits sometimes. Men can wear skirts, and it can be culturally expected sometimes for Scotsmen (kilts). Many African and Asian cultures have a wide range of clothing options for men and women that would seem inappropriate to European eyes. Muslim men often wear a long robe called a thawb (thobe, thaub, or thob). Judges, clergy, and professors frequently wear ceremonial robes as a sign of their respective positions.

The only legitimate case for fashion laws is to cover external primary reproductive organs (genitals) and elimination openings (urethra and anus), and even that is a cultural and public health choice and not empirically necessary.

This means that **legislation aimed at gender presentation is pointless.**

Marital Status

The intent behind encouraging marriage was to improve stability of relationships, but since the 1970's that has not been helpful.

Income tax was created by the 16th Amendment in 1916, but the concept of filing jointly didn't exist until 1948. [REF095] Women were considered property. Think of the marriage traditions of "giving away the bride" or a married woman taking the surname of her spouse. Who owned her before that? Her father? Does her partner own her after marriage?

Women didn't get the right to have credit cards and sign mortgages until 1974 with the Equal Credit Opportunity Act. [REF073] This and other legislation in that time period finally made it easier for women to live independently. As a result, **marriage is not needed for women to have financial stability and independence.**

Nevertheless, income tax, health insurance, and many other areas still make strong distinctions based on marital status. There is no longer government justification for this.

Sex and Gender Identity

Many "Christian" activists insist that the only human sexes are male and female, and everyone should be heterosexual (straight). These assumptions are purely culturally based (i.e., local opinions) and have no basis in history or science.

The author went into detail to describe how biology allows many more genetic chromosomes than just XX and XY, and issues with hormone creation and use can result in many people who have intersex conditions, making them defy the male-female binary. [REF070] Some of these conditions lead to formation of ambiguous genitals (not clearly male or female), which used to be called a hermaphrodite.

Some of these conditions are also seen in nature, such as birds or animals that are female on one lateral half, and male on the other half. These conditions can be called chimera or mosaic, depending on exactly how they originated. Other creatures can change their sex depending on environmental conditions or scarcity of one sex. This was hinted at in the first *Jurassic Park* movie (1993) [REF148] but is based on real science. The sex of many reptiles such as turtles and crocodilians depends on the temperature of the environment they mature in.

Technically, all cisgender men are transgender, because all fetuses start out female, but only start developing male or female organs (sexual differentiation) around 6-7 weeks' gestation. [REF004] Being female is the default for humans; it takes a lot of biological work to make someone male. That's why there is a clear seam down the middle of the scrotum and toward the anus – it would have become the vulva for a female.

Gender identity has a lot more options than just man or woman. People around the world have recognized for millennia people who didn't fit into that simple binary. Some Native Americans called them Two Spirit people or berdache, in India there are the Hijira, Bakla in the Philippines, and so on. [REF096] Transgender is an umbrella term for anyone who doesn't fit into the man/woman binary, and includes people who identify as pangender, cross-dressing, gender fluid, and more. (Figure 12)

The wide range of gender identities is very confusing for many people, because many of these labels have not been identified by Western science until the last few decades. People with these

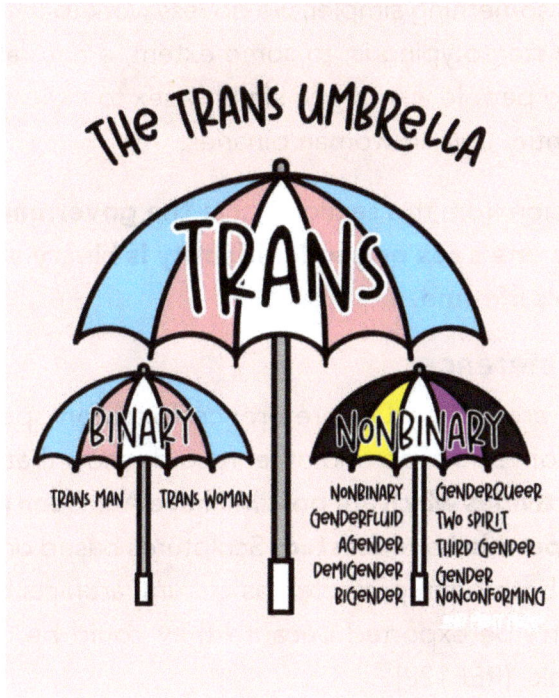

Figure 12. The Transgender Umbrella [REF127]

identities have always existed, we just didn't acknowledge that they existed. The term transgender was coined in 1965, [REF126] before that we mostly had just words for transsexuals (people who didn't agree with the sex they were assigned at birth) and transvestites (people who dressed as the opposite gender).

Why do people love to put sex and gender identity into simple binary (X or Y) choices? The answer lies in biology, but not between a person's legs. Survival has forced all organisms to live as efficiently as possible to be able to survive extreme conditions. In psychology this is sometimes called the "simplicity principle." [REF102]

One result of the simplicity principle is trying to reduce the amount of work our brains have to do. If we can take a complex topic and reduce it to something simpler, we do less work to think about it. That is why stereotyping is, to some extent, a natural tendency and leads to people wanting to simplify sex to male/female and gender identity to man/woman binaries.

The conclusion from this section is that **the government should not assume one's sex or gender identity is binary and is fixed during one's lifetime.**

Sexual Preference

Many laws around sexual preference focus on specific acts. Thousands of years of art and other records show that **the types of sexual activities which are possible have ALL been performed as long as people have existed.** Sculptures based on the Kama Sutra have both been protected as cultural artifacts but photos of them can't be exported because they could be considered pornographic. [REF128]

Assuming that we are dealing with people who are of age and mental competence to consent to sexual activity, **there is no reason for government to legislate sexual activities that are voluntary and consensual.** Activities outside that realm are addressed by rape, sexual assault, and pedophilia laws.

Technology Changes

A major challenge for technology laws is that some technology changes quickly. The 1979 Export Administration Act defined how fast a computer was to be considered a supercomputer and hence had strict "munitions" export regulations. [REF051] Bear in mind that at the time, a supercomputer could easily cost $10-15 million. By 1999, a Macintosh G4 desktop computer reached that supercomputer speed, and President Clinton had to change the export law. **It's hard to define a law specifically enough to achieve its purpose but not be quickly obsolete or overcome.**

That challenge is also seen in drug laws, where drugs which are illegal tend to be defined very precisely, but then a small change in formula can produce a new drug which does the same thing but is legal. This has been done for "designer drugs" for the recreational market, [REF005] and to evade patent laws for valuable prescription drugs. A new drug chemical composition resets the timeline for a patent being valid, which prevents anyone else producing a much cheaper generic version of it.

Not a legal issue, but an amusing technological change happened to both the Swedes and the Danes. Both tried to plan ahead responsibly in the early 19th century and planted thousands of trees to anticipate the need for building ships. Crafting a single warship could take 2,000 to 6,000 trees. The Swedes planted 300,000 oak trees starting in 1831, and the trees were deemed ready for harvest in 1975. [REF142] The Danes planted 90,000 oak trees in 1807, and they were ready in 2007. [REF143] By the time these "fleet oak" trees were ready for harvest, warships were no longer made of wood and hadn't been since around 1860. On the bright side, they made some lovely forests.

SUMMARY OF FEATURES

This sets the stage for the draft Constitution, which incorporates the changes justified in this section and many more.

- Fitness for Duty Assessments required for Executive, Legislative, and Judicial Branch candidates. Physical and mental health assessment, basic government knowledge, financial disclosure, and earned security clearances. Justices are exempt from security clearances.

- Term limits for Congress and Supreme Court (SC) of 12 years. Three-year terms for House. Eleven SC Justices. Justice recusal defined.

- Impeachment process defined for Congress and Supreme Court.

- Unlimited Congress size, one Representative for each state's 800,000 population, one Senator per state's 4 million population.

- Limit gerrymandering with the six-boundary rule for Electoral Districts.

- No PACs or SuperPACs, only individual contributions to campaigns. No insider trading or self-exemption from laws for Congress. No voter registration or voting fees.

- No Electoral College. Elect President & VP by simple majority vote.

- No corporate personhood (Citizens United).

- Explicit definition of separation of church and state, presumption of innocence, rule of law. Equal protection and equal rights under the law.

- No official language. Dual citizenship permitted.

- No incarceration for no cash bail when accused of non-violent crimes. Voting rights restored after incarceration. No death penalty or torture.

- Right to food, water, shelter for all.

- Healthcare – bodily autonomy defined. Universal healthcare.

- Equal Rights – no discrimination based on marriage, race, ethnicity, sexual preference, disability, gender identity, or gender presentation.

- Workers' rights defined for equal pay, right to unionize, and adequate rest.

- Education – universal public K-12 education with free meals during school hours. Free public college or trade schools for two years. No public funding for private or religious education.

- Territories must resolve status within 24 years.

- Mandate for consumer and environmental protection. Right to ethnic heritage.

ABOUT THE UNIFIED STATES CONSTITUTION

The draft Constitution which follows is not intended to be a complete finished product. It contains the key elements which are rewritten from the current US Constitution or are new. Some parts would have to be refined for legal accuracy. The document has been restructured extensively for clarity.

The original US Constitution has very long paragraphs which address many subjects, often in a single run-on sentence. The First Amendment defines five critical rights in one sentence. The first sentence in the 12th Amendment has over 200 words. Clearly few English teachers have been in Congress.

This Constitution uses military style dotted decimal paragraph numbers (e.g., 3.2.6) to make it easier to refer to a specific clause. The oddest part for the gentle reader may be that after '9' in a paragraph number, the next is '10', so 3.2.9, 3.2.10, 3.2.11, etc. This style makes it easier to add new clauses without changing the numbering of previous or later ones.

REFERENCES

This reference list is not intended to have formal academic citations, just provide proof that many of the statements are from sources other than the author.

---

001 | Attributed to Allen McCurdy, 1920, often revised by Native American and third-party proponents.

002 | https://abcnews.go.com/US/heres-learned-dojs-photo-classified-documents-mar-lago/story?id=89161286

003 | https://abcnews.go.com/US/inmate-firefighters-prisoners-deployed-battle-los-angeles-fires/story?id=117672530

004 | https://academic.oup.com/endo/article/142/8/3281/2988779

005 | https://americanaddictioncenters.org/designer-drugs-addiction

006 | https://api.army.mil/e2/c/downloads/568585.pdf

007 | https://apps.who.int/gho/data/node.main.HALE?lang=en

008 | https://bigthink.com/the-past/out-of-africa-events/

009 | https://blog.westminstercollection.com/2015/07/31/nine-kings-in-one-room-nine-great-european-currencies/

010 | https://cas.umw.edu/cprd/files/2011/09/Jefferson-Statute-2-versions.pdf

011 | https://case.edu/ech/articles/c/cuyahoga-river-fire

012 | https://constitution.congress.gov/constitution/amendment-22/

013 | https://constitutioncenter.org/media/files/constitution.pdf

014 | https://constitutioncenter.org/media/files/constitution.pdf

015 | https://ddlegio.com/

016 | https://deathpenaltyinfo.org/curriculum/high-school/about-the-death-penalty/history-of-the-death-penalty

017 | https://deathpenaltyinfo.org/database/innocence?race=Black

018 | https://dpic-cdn.org/production/documents/pdf/FactSheet.pdf

019 | https://dpic-cdn.org/production/documents/pdf/FactSheet.pdf

020 | https://en.wikipedia.org/wiki/1992_United_States_presidential_election

021 | https://en.wikipedia.org/wiki/2024_United_States_House_of_Representatives_elections_in_California

022 | https://en.wikipedia.org/wiki/Absolute_monarchy

023 | https://en.wikipedia.org/wiki/Cross-dressing_in_film_and_television

024 | https://en.wikipedia.org/wiki/Economic_system

025 | https://en.wikipedia.org/wiki/Executive_Order_12968

026 | https://en.wikipedia.org/wiki/Hijra_(South_Asia)

027 | https://en.wikipedia.org/wiki/History_of_cross-dressing

028 | https://en.wikipedia.org/wiki/Ilona_Staller

029 | https://en.wikipedia.org/wiki/In_God_We_Trust

030 | https://en.wikipedia.org/wiki/Jim_Crow_laws

031 | https://en.wikipedia.org/wiki/Left%E2%80%93right_political_spectrum

032 | https://en.wikipedia.org/wiki/List_of_forms_of_government

033 | https://en.wikipedia.org/wiki/List_of_infantry_weapons_in_the_American_Revolution

034 | https://en.wikipedia.org/wiki/List_of_U.S._states_and_territories_by_population

035 | https://en.wikipedia.org/wiki/Mormonism_and_polygamy

036 | https://en.wikipedia.org/wiki/Public_Works_Administration

037 | https://en.wikipedia.org/wiki/Scientific_racism

038 | https://en.wikipedia.org/wiki/Solomon

039 | https://en.wikipedia.org/wiki/State_(polity)

040 | https://en.wikipedia.org/wiki/Territories_of_the_United_States

041 | https://en.wikipedia.org/wiki/The_World%27s_Billionaires

042 | https://firstamendment.mtsu.edu/post/8th-circuit-in-god-we-trust-on-money-is-constitutional/

043 | https://fiscalnote.com/blog/how-old-118th-congress

044 | https://goopenva.org/authoring/720-influence-of-earlier-documents-on-the-constitution/view

045 | https://hcj.gov.ua/sites/default/files/field/file/the_constitution_of_ukraine.pdf 1

046 | https://highways.dot.gov/public-roads/summer-1996/federal-aid-highway-act-1956-creating-interstate-system

047 | https://history.house.gov/HistoricalHighlight/Detail/35159?ret=True

048 | https://interactives.ap.org/german-election-2025/german-election-results/

049 | https://journalofethics.ama-assn.org/article/should-nonhuman-animals-be-recognized-legally-persons/2024-09

050 | https://naacp.org/find-resources/history-explained/origins-modern-day-policing

051 | https://newsletter.pessimistsarchive.org/p/when-the-mac-was-a-munition

052 | https://perspectivesofchange.hms.harvard.edu/node/87

053 | https://philosophy.columbian.gwu.edu/sites/g/files/zaxdzs5446/files/2023-08/degrazia_elphantspersonhood.pdf

054 | https://pmc.ncbi.nlm.nih.gov/articles/PMC10376032/

055 | https://pubmed.ncbi.nlm.nih.gov/20443281/

056 | https://radicalmoderate.online/2024-general-election-part-2-the-great-divide/

057 | https://richardwaynegarganta.com/marriagetypes.htm

058 | https://scholarship.law.duke.edu/cgi/viewcontent.cgi?article=1561&context=lcp

059 | https://socialsciencepapers.wordpress.com/2013/01/01/gun-control/

060 | https://socialsciencepapers.wordpress.com/2013/08/07/position-paper-on-various-political-topics/

061 | https://socialsciencepapers.wordpress.com/2022/04/04/time-for-a-new-constitution/

062 | https://socialsciencepapers.wordpress.com/2023/03/07/not-just-xx-and-xy/

063 | https://socialsciencepapers.wordpress.com/2023/05/17/world-and-human-history-events/

064 | https://socialsciencepapers.wordpress.com/2024/06/24/political-terminology-and-buzzwords/

065 | https://socialsciencepapers.wordpress.com/2024/08/21/land-bridges-not-just-the-bering-strait/

066 | https://supreme.justia.com/cases/federal/us/118/394/

067 | https://thefulcrum.us/electoral-reforms/worst-gerrymandered-districts

068 | https://thesatanictemple.com/blogs/the-satanic-temple-tenets/there-are-seven-fundamental-tenets

069 | https://womenshistory.si.edu/blog/voices-independence-four-oral-histories-about-building-womens-economic-power

070 | https://wordpress.com/post/socialsciencepapers.wordpress.com/309

071 | https://www.acog.org/advocacy/facts-are-important/understanding-and-navigating-viability

072 | https://www.adamsmith.org/blog/who-was-wearing-the-trousers

073 | https://www.annenbergclassroom.org/resource/womens-rights/

074 | https://www.archives.gov/electoral-college/about

075 | https://www.archives.gov/files/press/press-kits/magna-carta/magna-carta-translation.pdf

076 | https://www.archives.gov/milestone-documents/14th-amendment

077 | https://www.battlefields.org/learn/articles/militia-minutemen-and-continentals-american-military-force-american-revolution

078 | https://www.biblegateway.com/passage/?search=Exodus%2021&version=NLT

079 | https://www.brennancenter.org/our-work/research-reports/roe-v-wade-and-supreme-court-abortion-cases

080 | https://www.britannica.com/topic/constitutional-monarchy

081 | https://www.businessinsider.com/comparing-wealth-of-each-founding-father-2020-6#john-hancock-8

082 | https://www.cabinetmagazine.org/issues/4/kastner.php

083 | https://www.census.gov/data/tables/2020/dec/2020-apportion-ment-data.html

084 | https://www.congress.gov/bill/117th-congress/house-bill/3684

085 | https://www.constituteproject.org/constitution/Norway_2014.pdf

086 | https://www.cpr.org/2024/10/24/elephants-personhood-human-rights-argument-cheyenne-mountain-zoo/

087 | https://www.directives.doe.gov/terms_definitions/restricted-data

088 | https://www.dol.gov/agencies/whd/child-labor

089 | https://www.engageny.org/file/2191/download/the_constitution_of_the_iroquois_nations.pdf

090 | https://www.fec.gov/legal-resources/court-cases/citizens-united-v-fec/

091 | https://www.findlaw.com/education/education-options/compul-sory-education-laws-background.html

092 | https://www.gao.gov/assets/gao-04-353r.pdf

093 | https://www.govinfo.gov/content/pkg/COMPS-748/pdf/COMPS-748.pdf

094 | https://www.gp.org/ten_key_values

095 | https://www.hrblock.com/tax-center/filing/personal-tax-planning/how-filing-jointly-came-to-be/

096 | https://www.hrc.org/news/two-spirit-and-lgbtq-idenitites-today-and-centuries-ago

097 | https://www.imdb.com/title/tt0094291/?ref_=nv_sr_srsg_3_tt_8_nm_0_in_0_q_wall%2520street

098 | https://www.imdb.com/title/tt0364845/?ref_=fn_all_ttl_1

099 | https://www.imdb.com/title/tt0387808/

100 | https://www.nature.com/scitable/topicpage/human-evolutionary-tree-417/

101 | https://www.ncbi.nlm.nih.gov/pmc/articles/PMC2885717/

102 | https://www.ncbi.nlm.nih.gov/pmc/articles/PMC5125387/

103 | https://www.ncc.brent.sch.uk/attachments/download.asp?file=1446&type=pdf

104 | https://www.ncsl.org/elections-and-campaigns/campaign-contribution-limits-overview

105 | https://www.newcastlecastle.co.uk/castle-blog/wedding

106 | https://www.oed.com/dictionary/kakistocracy_n?tl=true

107 | https://www.opensecrets.org/news/2023/01/federal-lobbying-spending-reaches-4-1-billion-in-2022-the-highest-since-2010/

108 | https://www.outdoorlife.com/photos/gallery/guns/rifles/2011/06/21-worst-gun-laws-ever/

109 | https://www.peosoldier.army.mil/Equipment/Equipment-Portfolio/Project-Manager-Soldier-Lethality-Portfolio/M107-Semi-Automatic-Long-Range-Sniper-Rifle/

110 | https://www.pewresearch.org/religion/2024/01/24/religious-nones-in-america-who-they-are-and-what-they-believe/

111 | https://www.quorum.us/data-driven-insights/who-are-the-longest-serving-members-of-congress/

112 | https://www.schneier.com/blog/archives/2006/08/security_is_a_t.html

113 | https://www.science.org/content/article/jews-and-arabs-share-recent-ancestry

114 | https://www.senate.gov/artandhistory/history/civil_rights/civil_rights.htm

115 | https://www.statnews.com/2023/11/13/life-expectancy-men-women/

116 | https://www.supremecourt.gov/about/faq_justices.aspx

117 | https://www.theatlantic.com/ideas/archive/2019/11/electoral-college-racist-origins/601918/

118 | https://www.tribal-institute.org/2014/INCTwo-SpiritBooklet.pdf

119 | https://www.un.org/en/udhrbook/pdf/udhr_booklet_en_web.pdf

120 | https://www.uni-goettingen.de/en/650077.html

121 | https://www.uptodate.com/contents/calculator-estimated-date-of-delivery-edd-patient-education

122 | https://www.usa.gov/campaign-finance-laws

123 | https://www.usatoday.com/story/news/politics/2023/02/10/how-many-justices-supreme-court-list-justices-2023/10796688002/

124 | https://www.vera.org/news/the-chains-of-slavery-still-exist-in-mass-incarceration

125 | https://www2.census.gov/library/publications/decennial/1990/population-of-states-and-counties-us-1790-1990/population-of-states-and-counties-of-the-united-states-1790-1990.pdf

126 | https://en.wikipedia.org/wiki/Transsexual

127 | https://www.facebook.com/TransgenderLighthouse

128 | https://en.wikipedia.org/wiki/Kama_Sutra

129 | https://en.wikipedia.org/wiki/Caucasian_race

130 | https://www.spolinlaw.com/blog/2022/11/09/what-is-a-commutation-of-sentence-how-to-win/

131 | https://www.imdb.com/title/tt0104990/

132 | https://www.bls.gov/opub/mlr/2017/article/history-of-child-labor-in-the-united-states-part-1.htm

133 | https://news.lib.wvu.edu/2018/09/05/before-the-holiday-remembering-child-labor-in-west-virginia/

134 | https://www.digitaltransgenderarchive.net/learn/terms

135 | https://today.usc.edu/pink-for-boys-and-blue-for-girls-the-colorful-history-of-things-designed-for-kids/

136 | https://www.folger.edu/blogs/shakespeare-and-beyond/the-first-english-actresses/

137 | https://www.ncsl.org/elections-and-campaigns/voter-id

138 | https://en.wikipedia.org/wiki/Metric_prefix

139 | https://docs.house.gov/meetings/GO/GO00/20220929/115171/HHRG-117-GO00-20220929-SD010.pdf

140 | https://www.facebook.com/revealedhistory on April 9, 2025

141 | https://home.nra.org/

142 | https://en.wikipedia.org/wiki/Visings%C3%B6

143 | https://www.avalanchepress.com/Danish_Navy.php

144 | https://www.brennancenter.org/sites/default/files/analysis/Briefing_Memo_Debunking_Voter_Fraud_Myth.pdf

145 | https://en.wikipedia.org/wiki/Robert_A._Heinlein

146 | https://www.atf.gov/file/55391/download

147 | https://law.justia.com/cases/federal/appellate-courts/ca2/23-793/23-793-2024-12-30.html

148 | https://www.imdb.com/title/tt0107290/?ref_=nv_sr_srsg_0_tt_8_nm_0_in_0_q_jurassic

CONSTITUTION

for the

UNIFIED STATES OF AMERICA

PREAMBLE

This Constitution defines a democratic government that tolerates capitalism but moderates unabashed greed. It states explicit assumptions about fundamental human rights, core legal principles, and the role of the country in the world to prevent corruption by antidemocratic forces.

Drawing inspiration from governments from the 13th to the 21st centuries CE, this Constitution defines the structure, functions, assumptions, and constraints on the government for the Unified States of America. Critical features include term limits and Fitness for Duty assessments for all high-level government positions, and a novel way to limit electoral gerrymandering.

ARTICLE 0 – FOUNDING PRINCIPLES

This Constitution is based on making critical assumptions about the purpose of government, the nature of humanity and our relationship with nature, and the role of citizens and residents in government.

Section 0.1 – Life

All people have the right to life, freedom, security of person, and the pursuit of happiness. All human beings are born free and equal in dignity and rights.

The human being, their life and health, honor and dignity, inviolability and security shall be recognized as the highest social value.

In the exercise of their rights and freedoms, everyone shall be subject only to such limitations as are determined by law solely for the purpose of securing due recognition and respect for the rights and freedoms of others and of meeting the just requirements of morality, public order and the general welfare in a democratic society.

Section 0.2 – Fallibility

People are fallible. When a person makes a mistake, they should be given the opportunity to rectify it, resolve or mitigate any harm caused, and prevent repeating that mistake, all without judicial intervention when possible.

Section 0.3 – Personal Dignity and Actualization

Everyone has the right to a secure society in which they may have dignity and develop their personality to meet their economic, intellectual, artistic, social and/or cultural goals.

Social life shall be based on the principles of political, economic, and ideological diversity.

Section 0.4 – Government Purpose

Government is a set of structures and rules to improve the safety and happiness of our citizens and residents and guide our interaction with other States.

Section 0.5 – Legislative Purpose

The government shall enact and enforce laws to ensure that the structures and functions of the State are utilized and administered in the best interests of the general public.

The people shall be the bearer of sovereignty and the sole source of power. The people shall exercise power directly and through the government authorities and local government.

Section 0.6 – Punishment Authority

The State is the sole authority to define fiscal and/or physical punishments or restriction of other rights.

Section 0.7 – Role in Nature

Humanity is an integral part of nature, including the Earth, our solar system, galaxy, and universe. Humans are caretakers of the Earth.

People should strive to act with compassion and empathy toward all creatures in accordance with reasonable need for survival. Policies and goals shall be made to create a culture and society which is sustainable for many generations.

ARTICLE 1 – INTRODUCTION

The goal of this Constitution is to define a democratic republic State which will meet the needs of all of its citizens, residents, and visitors and be a responsible proponent of democracy in the world.

Section 1.1 – Inspiration for this Constitution

Sources of inspiration for this document include the Constitution of the United States of America [REF01], the Constitution of the Ukraine as of 4/26/2023 [REF04], the Seven Tenets of the Satanic Temple [REF03], Norway's Constitution of 1814 with Amendments through 2014 [REF06], the Green Party Ten Key Values [REF08], the Magna Carta of 1215 [REF05], and the Constitution of the Iroquois Nations, circa 1500 [REF07]. Other sources include fundamental definitions from political science and the imagination of the author.

Section 1.2 – Branches of Government

The government shall consist of Executive, Legislative, and Judicial Branches which are coequal and provide checks and balances on each other's authority and actions. As coequal branches, they must not attempt to control or unduly influence each other's authority and actions.

Executive, Legislative, and Judicial authorities shall exercise their powers within the limits established by this Constitution and in accordance with the laws of the Unified States.

No law enforcement agent or agency shall act as a judicial officer.

Section 1.3 – Type of Government

The Unified States of America are based on a representative democracy.

The Unified States of America are a sovereign and independent, democratic, social, law-based State.

Section 1.4 – Type of Economy

The Unified States of America's economy is based on capitalism, with the government exercising necessary controls to prevent abuses of workers, product and/or service pricing, or unfair control of vertical and/or horizontal markets.

Everyone in the Unified States shall have the right to entrepreneurial activity that is not prohibited by law.

Section 1.5 – International Relations Goals

A key objective of the Unified States of America globally is to encourage and support the development and flourishing of other States which are based on democratic principles and honor human rights.

Foreign political activity shall be aimed at ensuring its national interests and security by maintaining peaceful and mutually beneficial co-operation with members of the international community according to the generally acknowledged principles and norms of international law.

Section 1.6 – Property Ownership

Every citizen and resident has the right to own property, alone as well as in association with others.

No one may be deprived of property by the State except in accordance with relevant criminal conviction.

Section 1.7 – Duties of the People

The will of the people (citizens, residents, and visitors) is the basis of authority for the government.

The people are expected to resolve conflicts with non-violent means whenever possible, while also respecting the need for personal safety.

The people are encouraged to communicate their unmet legislative needs and desires through local, state, and federal government legislators.

Citizens and residents have the right to participate in government, directly and/or through representation.

Citizens and residents are expected to hold their representatives accountable to their respective oaths of office in accordance with this Constitution.

ARTICLE 2 – EXECUTIVE BRANCH

The Executive Branch consists of the Offices of the President, Vice President, and the Armed Forces.

Section 2.1 – Office of the President

The President shall be the highest Executive officer of the government. The President is responsible for all actions by the Executive Branch.

2.1.1 – Define President's Cabinet

The Office of the President shall include a Cabinet, each of which contains Secretaries for each major policy area: Secretaries of Commerce, Defense (including Veterans' Affairs), Education, Energy, Health and Human Services, Housing, Interior (including Agriculture), Justice, Labor, State, Transportation, and Treasury. The role of these Secretaries is to manage their respective policy areas and advise the President on policy decisions and resource desires relevant to their area of expertise.

2.1.2 – President Qualifications

The President shall be at least thirty-five (35) years of age when assuming office. They must be a citizen of the Unified States for at least five (5) years. They must pass Fitness for Duty assessments as described in Section 6.7.

2.1.3 – President Election and Term of Office

The President shall be elected by a simple majority of the popular vote and serve a term of four (4) years. In the event an election does not result in a clear majority (>50% of votes cast), the election will be repeated thirty (30) days later with the three candidates with the most votes until a majority is obtained.

The President can serve no more than two (2) terms, consecutively or not.

2.1.4 – Removal of President

The President may step down temporarily in the event of medical or psychological illness or other personal issue. The Vice President will act on their behalf during that time.

The President can be permanently removed from office (impeachment) by 60% majority vote of both the House and Senate for: treason, permanent incapacity, or unexplained absence of more than a week. In that event, the Line of Succession is applied.

2.1.5 – President Responsibilities and Powers

Presidential duties include definition of foreign policy, economic policy, and vision for the future of the State and her people. The President represents, serves, and is a civil servant for all of the people in the Unified States, regardless of political affiliation or personal ideology.

The President is Supreme Commander of the Office of the Armed Forces and collaborates with the Military Master to determine objectives for military force strength, projection, and actions.

The President may authorize foreign military action not to exceed fourteen (14) days. Longer engagements require a formal declaration of war by the Senate.

The President may pardon people for Federal offenses. Candidates for pardon must first be vetted and approved by at least three (3) National Supreme Court justices. No one may be pardoned for treason or impeachment.

The President nominates National Supreme Court justices for Senate approval.

The President may make treaties or other international agreements, with sixty percent (60%) of the Senate concurring.

The President may appoint Ambassadors to other States. Such appointments may last up to six (6) years, consecutive or not.

The President shall give a State of the Union address at least annually to convey accomplishments, challenges, and objectives for their Administration.

The President shall sign or veto legislation written by the House and approved by the House and Senate within thirty (30) calendar days of being presented with it. The Senate may override a Presidential veto with a two-thirds (2/3) majority vote.

Section 2.2 – Office of the Vice President

The Vice President shall represent the President in domestic and international affairs to the extent determined by the President.

2.2.1 – Vice President Qualifications

The Vice President shall be at least thirty-five (35) years of age when assuming office. They must be a citizen of the Unified States for at least five (5) years.

They must pass Fitness for Duty assessments as described in Section 6.7.

No one may be Vice President who is not qualified to be President.

2.2.2 – Vice President Election and Term of Office

The Vice President is elected with the President. The Vice President may serve no more than two (2) terms, consecutively or not, regardless of the President(s) with whom they serve.

2.2.3 – Removal of Vice President

The Vice President may be removed from office temporarily or permanently under the same criteria as the President. In that event, the Line of Succession is applied.

2.2.4 – Vice President Responsibilities and Powers

The Vice President is an advisor to the President and represents the President for diplomatic or policy events which the President does not attend.

The Vice President is a non-voting presiding officer of the Senate when the Chief Senator is not available to serve in that capacity.

The Vice President is first in the Line of Succession in the event the President is no longer able to fulfill their duties, either temporarily or permanently.

Section 2.3 – Office of the Armed Forces

The purpose of this Office is to protect the Unified States from foreign and domestic threats and support allied countries in accordance with relevant treaties, Non-Government Organizations (NGO), and alliances such as the United Nations, NATO, etc.

The defense of the Unified States and protection of its sovereignty, territorial integrity and inviolability shall be entrusted to the Office of the Armed Forces.

The Armed Forces and other military formations shall not be used by anyone to restrict the rights and freedoms of citizens or with the intent to overthrow the constitutional order, subvert the government authorities or obstruct their activities.

The Armed Forces are sworn to uphold this Constitution, not the President or any other person, association, or political party.

2.3.1 – Define Military Master

The Office of the Armed Forces is led by the Military Master, who reports to the President.

The Military Master is appointed by the President and must be an Officer from one of the Armed Forces Departments. They must pass Fitness for Duty assessments as described in Section 6.7.

The Military Master may serve no more than twelve (12) years, consecutively or not.

2.3.2 – Armed Forces Departments

The Office of the Armed Forces include Departments for protection of coastal boundaries, land, sea, and air. This Office also manages veterans' benefits.

2.3.3 – Define Department Secretaries

Each Armed Forces Department is led by a Secretary who guides the policy and goals of their Department in coordination with the Military Master.

Each Secretary approves promotion of high-ranking officers within their Department.

2.3.4 – Required Military Service

The Military Master shall advise the President when military conscription is recommended, and define the resources needed to meet strategic and mission objectives. Conscription may be ordered by the President, with simple majority approval by the Senate, for a period not to exceed two (2) years, upon which its need will be reevaluated.

All citizens are subject to conscription from the age of majority to an age stated in the order by the President. All sexes may be conscripted. People who are physically or mentally unable, and/or have moral objections to military service, may be assigned non-combat, non-violent support roles.

2.3.5 – Veterans' Affairs

The Office of the Armed Forces is responsible for providing the pension, physical and mental healthcare, and continuing education of personnel after they have completed their service commitment(s) honorably. The extent of these services shall be defined in writing at the start of their service, and typically will depend on their years of service, military status or rank, and retirement plan.

Section 2.4 – Line of Succession

If the President and Vice President are both unable to perform their duties, the Chief Senator will become acting President, and the Chief Representative will become acting Vice President. The House and Senate will each vote on temporary Chief leadership, respectively.

After the Chief Representative, the Line of Succession is the Secretary of State, the Secretary of Defense, and the Attorney General to act as President. The acting Vice President shall be the next person in the Line of Succession after the acting President.

If deeper Line of Succession candidates are needed, the House and Senate shall vote for acting President and Vice President from current members of Congress. The votes from both parts of Congress shall be added and the person with most votes shall be acting President, the person with second most votes shall be acting Vice President.

The acting President and/or Vice President shall fulfill those roles until the elected people in those roles resume service, or until the next election.

ARTICLE 3 – LEGISLATIVE BRANCH

The Legislative Branch shall consist of two (2) parts, the House of Representatives and the Senate. Together they constitute Congress.

Section 3.1 – The House of Representatives

The House shall consist of Representatives who each represent the people within one (1) Electoral District.

3.1.1 – House Purpose

The purpose of the House of Representatives is to draft and approve State laws to serve the needs of the people of the Unified States. Each Representative should serve both the needs of their Electoral District as well as weigh the impact on the overall State.

The House may define Committees to develop and approve early drafts of proposed legislation. Once approved by its Committee, draft legislation must be presented to the full House for review and vote within thirty (30) working days.

The House is responsible for drafting and approving the Federal Budget. The Budget is presented to the President for approval or veto. Amendment or line-item veto of the Federal Budget by the President is not permitted.

The House may vote to impeach the President and/or Vice President for treason, bribery, or intentional violation of the oath of office by a two-thirds (2/3) majority. There is no appeal for impeachment.

3.1.2 – Electoral Districts Scope

Each Electoral District shall have no more than a population of eight hundred thousand (800,000) people upon its creation.

The number of Electoral Districts shall be redefined on the basis of a complete National Census. Each state shall have at least one (1) Electoral District.

The total number of Electoral Districts, and hence the total number of Representatives, is not fixed.

3.1.3 – Electoral District Boundaries Defined

Each Electoral District shall be defined by no more than six (6) geographic boundaries. Each geographic boundary of an Electoral District shall only be one of the following:

- The centerline of a named street (avenue, boulevard, road, etc.),

- A line of fixed latitude or longitude,

- A county, state, or national (State) boundary,

- The middle of a moving body of water (river, stream, creek, etc.), or

- The shore of a lake, sea, gulf, or ocean.

3.1.4 – Representative Qualifications

Each Representative shall be at least thirty (30) years old when assuming office. They must be a citizen for at least five (5) years. They must pass Fitness for Duty assessments as described in Section 6.7.

Each Representative must be a resident of the Electoral District they represent for at least one (1) calendar year before assuming office and throughout their term(s) of service.

3.1.5 – Representative Term

Representatives serve a term of three (3) years. They may serve no more than four (4) terms, consecutively or not. In the event a Representative cannot complete their term of service, their seat shall remain vacant until the next election.

3.1.6 – House Chief Representative Defined

The House shall be led by a Chief Representative, who is elected by the Representatives at the start of each session by simple majority. Each session lasts three (3) years, and one half (1/2) of Representatives are elected before each session.

The Chief Representative presides over House activities and determines the order in which Committee-approved legislation shall be considered by the full House.

Section 3.2 – The Senate

3.2.1 – Senate Purpose

The Senate functions as a longer-term governing body, like a corporation's board of directors.

The purpose of the Senate is to review and approve (or veto) bills passed by the House by simple majority. Bills which are approved are given to the President for signature or veto.

The Senate drafts and approves international agreements or treaties by simple majority.

The Senate approves candidates for the National Supreme Court.

The Senate approves military conscription requested by the President and Military Master.

3.2.2 – Number of Senators

Each state shall have one Senator per four million (4,000,000) population, rounded up. Each state shall have at least one (1) Senator. This number is adjusted based on each National Census.

The total number of Senators is not fixed.

States with more than one (1) Senator shall determine which Electoral Districts belong to each Senator, with goals of having a similar number of adjacent Electoral Districts and similar population represented by each Senator.

3.2.3 – Senator Qualifications

Senators must be at least thirty-five (35) years old when assuming office. They must be a citizen for at least five (5) years. They must pass Fitness for Duty assessments as described in Section 6.7.

Senators must be a resident of the state they represent for at least one (1) calendar year before assuming office and throughout their term(s) of service.

3.2.4 – Senator Term

Senators serve a term of six (6) years. They may serve no more than two (2) terms, consecutive or not.

In the event a Senator cannot complete their term of service, their seat shall remain vacant until the next election.

3.2.5 – Chief Senator Defined

The Senate shall be led by a Chief Senator, who is elected by the Senators at the start of each session by a simple majority. Each session lasts three (3) years, and one half (1/2) of Senators are elected before each session.

The Chief Senator presides over Senate sessions and determines the order in which House-approved legislation is addressed. In the event the Chief Senator is not available, the Vice President shall preside over the Senate as a non-voting member.

Section 3.3 – Congress Impeachment

Members of the House or Senate may be impeached by a two-thirds (2/3) majority vote by the opposite part of Congress, i.e., a House member may be impeached by the Senate, or *vice versa*. Impeachment may be on the basis of permanent incapacity, unexplained absence of more than a week, willful violation of the oath of office, or felony conviction.

Impeachment shall result in immediate removal of the legislator from their position, and disqualification from serving in the Executive or Legislative Branches in the future. There is no appeal for impeachment.

ARTICLE 4 – JUDICIAL BRANCH

The Judicial Branch consists of the National Supreme Court and the State Supreme Courts. Additional levels of jurisprudence shall be defined as needed by legislation.

Section 4.1 – National Supreme Court

The National Supreme Court is the highest judicial authority in the country.

The National Supreme Court has original jurisdiction for cases between states, cases involving Ambassadors, cases involving maritime boundaries, and cases involving Unified States citizens or residents versus other States.

The National Supreme Court has appellate jurisdiction for cases that were ruled upon by a State Supreme Court and appealed or were beyond the scope of a State Supreme Court.

4.1.1 – National Supreme Court Justice Qualifications

Justices on the National Supreme Courts must be at least thirty-five (35) years of age when assuming office. They must be a citizen of the Unified States for at least three (3) years and be recognized as a lawyer by a state. They must pass Fitness for Duty assessments as described in Section 6.7.

A National Supreme Court Justice may not belong to political parties or trade unions, take part in any political activity, hold a representative mandate, hold any other paid offices, or perform other remunerated work except for research, teaching, or creative activities.

4.1.2 – National Supreme Court Justice Term

National Supreme Court Justices serve a single term of twelve (12) years.

4.1.3 – National Supreme Court Justice Selection

National Supreme Court justices are nominated by the President and must be approved by a simple majority of the Senate AND a simple majority of the House.

There shall be eleven (11) National Supreme Court justices.

Section 4.2 – State Supreme Courts

The role of State Supreme Courts is to rule on lower court decisions which have been appealed or are beyond their scope. The key criteria to be applied are whether the lower court decisions are consistent with Federal, State, and local laws. The State Supreme Courts may also need to resolve cases of conflicting rights between jurisdictions within a state.

4.2.1 – State Supreme Court Justice Qualifications

Justices for the State Supreme Courts must be at least thirty (30) years of age when assuming office. They must be a citizen of the Unified States for at least three (3) years and be recognized as a lawyer by the State they represent. They must pass Fitness for Duty assessments as described in Section 6.7.

A State Supreme Court Justice may not belong to political parties or trade unions, take part in any political activity, hold a representative mandate, hold any other paid offices, or perform other remunerated work except for research, teaching, or creative activities.

4.2.2 – State Supreme Court Justice Term

State Supreme Court Justices serve a single term of twelve (12) years.

4.2.3 – State Supreme Court Justice Selection

State Supreme Court justices are nominated by the Governor of their state and must be approved by a simple majority of the Senate.

Each state shall have eleven (11) State Supreme Court justices.

Section 4.3 – Core Legal Principles

4.3.1 – Rule of Law

The rule of law shall be recognized and effective in the Unified States. The Constitution shall be regarded as the highest law.

Laws and amendments which are derived from or added to this Constitution shall be consistent with this Constitution.

The legal order shall be based on the principles according to which no one may be forced to do what is not stipulated by law.

Citizens, residents, and visitors of the Unified States shall be obliged to abide strictly by the Constitution and laws of the Unified States, and not to encroach upon the rights, freedoms, honor, or dignity of other people.

Ignorance of laws shall not exempt anyone from legal liability.

4.3.2 – Personhood

The legal start of a person's rights is at live birth and continues indefinitely after death.

Before birth, a fetus is the responsibility of the parent carrying them. Laws may not be applied against a fetus.

Personhood only applies to members of the species *Homo sapiens sapiens*, i.e., human beings.

4.3.3 – Voting Rights

All citizens of the Unified States of America have the universal and equal right to vote for elected local, city, state, and federal (State) candidates, provided they are not currently incarcerated.

Voting shall be by secret ballot or other equivalent procedures.

No fee may be required or implied for registering to vote or voting.

Anonymized records of votes cast shall be kept for a minimum of twenty-five (25) years.

4.3.4 – Immunity from Prosecution

No one shall be obliged to execute rulings or orders that are manifestly criminal. If needed, the courts shall resolve whether a ruling or order is manifestly criminal.

The President and Vice President may not be prosecuted during their term, except for treason and/or impeachment. The statute of limitations for other charged crimes shall resume after they leave office.

4.3.5 – Martial Law

Martial law may only be enacted by the President with unanimous witnessed consensus in writing of the Vice President, House Chief Representative, and Chief Senator.

Under the conditions of martial law or a state of emergency, specific restrictions on rights and freedoms may be established with the indication of the period of effect for such restrictions. Personal rights 5.1.1 through 5.1.6 may not be restricted even under martial law.

4.3.6 – Treason Defined

Treason is defined as 1) levying War against these Unified States, and/or 2) supporting the Enemies of the Unified States, such as providing them with financial support, materiel support, and/or encouraging them to act against these Unified States.

Treason may be charged against any person in the State or citizens who live abroad.

4.3.7 – Air and Sea Boundaries

Air space for the Unified States is defined as up to the internationally recognized Kármán line, 100 km above sea level. [REF12] Above that line is legally considered outer space, and subject to appropriate international law and treaties.

Maritime boundaries shall be defined in accordance with international law and negotiated with neighboring States as needed. [REF11]

4.3.8 – Single State

No other State(s) shall exist within the boundaries of the Unified States.

Section 4.4 – Pretrial Rights

4.4.1 – No Arbitrary Arrest or Custody

No one shall be subjected to arbitrary arrest, detention or exile.

No one shall be arrested or held in custody except under a substantiated court decision and on the grounds and in accordance with the procedure established by law.

4.4.2 – Presumption of Innocence

All people are assumed innocent of a crime until convicted of said crime. No one shall be subjected to criminal punishment until his/her guilt is proved through a legal procedure and established by a court verdict of guilty.

4.4.3 – No Self Incrimination

No person may be forced to testify against themselves.

4.4.4 – Right to Representation

Every person, arrested or detained, shall be informed without delay of the reasons for their arrest or detention, apprised of their rights, and from the moment of detention, given an opportunity to personally defend themself or to receive legal aid from a defender.

4.4.5 – Proportional Bail

The amount of bail shall be fair for the crimes accused and not excessive.

Bail amounts may be adjusted according to the defendant's socioeconomic status.

No defendant may be held before trial for non-violent crimes if they cannot produce cash bail.

Section 4.5 – Trial Rights

4.5.1 – Right to Trial

Everyone is entitled in full equality to a fair and public trial by an independent and impartial court, in the determination of their rights and obligations and of any criminal charge against them.

No one shall be held guilty of any penal offence on account of any act or omission which did not constitute a penal offence at the time when it was committed. Nor shall a heavier penalty be imposed than the one that was applicable at the time the penal offence was committed. (No *ex post facto* laws.)

No bill of attainder is allowed.

4.5.2 – No Double Jeopardy

No person may be prosecuted twice for the same crime at the same level of jurisdiction.

4.5.3 - Judicial Decisions

Judicial decisions and laws should be based on the best scientific understanding of the world, while also recognizing that scientific understanding changes over time. Everyone shall take care never to distort scientific facts to fit one's biases, preconceived notions, or personal objectives.

Judicial decisions and laws should also be based on respect for human rights and the psychological, emotional, spiritual, and philosophical needs of the people.

4.5.4 - Speedy Trial

Criminal prosecutions for state crimes shall be held in the Electoral District in which the alleged crimes occurred. Criminal prosecutions for State crimes shall be held in the state in which the alleged crimes occurred. If a criminal activity allegedly occurred in more than one Electoral District or state, the jurisdiction of its origin shall be used.

Trials shall be public and use an impartial jury of peers for major offenses. Lesser offenses may be adjudicated by a judge without a jury.

Witnesses for the prosecution and the defense may be presented.

Every defendant is entitled to have qualified counsel to aid in their defense.

4.5.5 - Right to Appeal

Defendants have the right to appeal a verdict to higher courts. The National Supreme Court is the highest possible level of appeal after lower courts have been exhausted.

Appeals to the court in defense of the constitutional rights and freedoms of the individual and citizen directly on the grounds of the Constitution shall be guaranteed (writ of *habeas corpus*).

Everyone has the right to an effective remedy by the competent National Supreme Court for acts violating the fundamental rights granted them by the Constitution or by law.

Section 4.6 – Punishment Rights

Punishment imposed by criminal conviction shall be fair and reasonable for the crimes committed. Punishment must be consistent regardless of defendant's race, ethnicity, marital status, disability, sexual orientation, sex, gender identity, or gender presentation.

A convicted person shall enjoy all human and civil rights except for the restrictions determined by law and established by a court verdict.

4.6.1 – No Collective or Kin Punishment

No law may incarcerate or fine the family members of a person who is convicted.

No law may incarcerate or fine a group of people for the actions of a few.

No law may punish the descendants of a person or otherwise extend punishment beyond the lifespan of the person convicted.

4.6.2 – No Capital Punishment or Torture

No law may punish a person by death. No one shall be arbitrarily deprived of life.

Incarceration may be allowed until death of the person.

No one shall be subjected to torture or to cruel, inhuman or degrading treatment or punishment.

Section 4.7 - Recusal of Justices

National and State Supreme Court Justices shall recuse themselves from every case in which they have a perceived or real conflict of interest.

Conflicts of interest may include but are not limited to: substantial investment in one or more of the case's parties, having worked with or under one or more of the parties, having represented one or more of the case's parties outside of the National or State Courts, or having any of those conflicts through a close family member.

Section 4.8 - Impeachment of Justices

National and State Supreme Court Justices can be impeached for failure to disclose significant conflicts of interest, failure to respect core legal principles, or treason.

Impeachment of Justices requires a sixty percent (60%) majority vote by both House and Senate. There is no appeal for impeachment.

ARTICLE 5 – BILL OF RIGHTS

Section 5.1 – Personal Rights

5.1.1 – Equal Rights Statement

Equality of rights under the law shall not be denied or abridged by the Unified States or by any state or local government on account of race, ethnicity, marital status, disability, sexual orientation, sex, gender identity, or gender presentation.

Collection of personal data on any of the above characteristics shall only be allowed for demographic or public health purposes.

5.1.2 – Survival Rights

The citizens and residents of the Unified States of America have a fundamental right to adequate shelter, potable water, and food.

5.1.3 – Right to Healthcare

Every person in the Unified States shall have the right to healthcare, including medical, dental, vision, and mental health care.

Health protection shall be ensured through state funding of the relevant socio-economic, medical and sanitary, health improvement and prevention programs.

No person shall be subjected to medical, scientific or other experiments without free and informed consent.

5.1.4 – Right to Bodily Autonomy

A person's body is inviolable, subject to one's own will alone. The people of the Unified States of America have a fundamental right to bodily autonomy.

5.1.5 – Freedom from Religion

The people in the Unified States have the right to freedom of religion and freedom from religion. No law shall discriminate based on a person's religion, faith, spirituality, or absence thereof.

The people have the right to freedom of personal philosophy and religion. This right shall include the freedom to profess any religion or profess no religion, to freely practice religious rites and ceremonial rituals, alone or collectively, and to pursue religious activities.

The exercise of this right may be restricted by law only to protect the public order, health and morality of the population, or to protect the rights and freedoms of other people.

5.1.6 – Equal Protection

All are equal before the law and are entitled without any discrimination to equal protection of the law.

5.1.7 – Personal Movement

Everyone has the right to freedom of movement and residence within the borders of each state.

Everyone has the right to leave any State, including their own, and to return to their State. This right may not be invoked to evade punishment for non-political crimes.

5.1.8 – Marriage

Marriage is defined as a committed intentional relationship between two or more free and consenting adults or emancipated minors.

A marriage may be acknowledged by the State, but has no specific privileges associated with it.

5.1.9 – Workers' Rights

Everyone has the right to work in the field of their choosing in favorable conditions.

Everyone has the right to equal pay for equal work.

Everyone has the right to earn adequate pay for dignified existence.

Everyone has the right to form and join trade or other labor unions to protect their interests.

Everyone has the right to rest and leisure time, including a reasonable limit on working hours.

5.1.10 – No Slavery

No one shall be held in slavery or servitude. Slavery and the slave trade shall be prohibited in all their forms.

Incarcerated people shall not be forced to work. Their work must be compensated fairly.

5.1.11 – Right to Heritage

Everyone has the right to learn about their ethnic and cultural heritage, traditions, rituals, language, and history. Practice of their traditions and rituals, and speaking native languages are protected free speech.

Cultural heritage shall be protected by law.

5.1.12 – Consumer Protection

The State shall ensure the protection of competition in entrepreneurial activity. The abuse of a monopolistic position in the market, unlawful restriction of competition, and unfair competition shall not be permitted. The types and limits of monopolies shall be determined by law.

The State shall protect the rights of consumers, exercise control over the quality and safety of products and all types of services and works and promote the activities of public consumer associations.

5.1.13 – Environmental Protection

Everyone shall have the right to an environment that is safe for life and health and to compensation for damages caused by violation of this right.

5.1.14 – Parenthood Rights

Parent(s) shall sustain their children until they are adults or petition successfully for emancipation. This right may be released if the parents are deemed incapable by a court or give up their children for adoption.

Children have equal rights regardless of the marital status of their parent(s).

Parents and/or their child may be responsible for the actions of the child depending on the child's age, maturity, and the severity of the actions. The minimum age for criminal responsibility is not fixed for all children.

5.1.15 – Children's Work Rights

Children have the right to work if they so choose, provided that the amount and schedule of work do not interfere with adequate time for education, rest, and social interaction. Parental consent is required for children under the age of fourteen (14) years to work.

Section 5.2 – Communication Rights

5.2.1 – Free Speech

Every person in the Unified States shall have the right of free speech, with exceptions for treason, endangering others, or violation of other personal rights.

5.2.2 – Freedom of Media

The free press is necessary for the exchange of ideas. The press in this context includes printed, electronic, computer (internet), electromagnetic (television, radio), or other media formats.

Censorship shall be prohibited except where it violates free speech.

5.2.3 – Right to Assembly and Association

Every person in the Unified States shall have the right to assemble peacefully and belong to association(s).

No one may be forced to belong to an association.

All lawful associations of citizens and residents shall be equal before the law.

Associations and political parties may be ruled illegal by a court if their goals and/or actions violate this Constitution.

5.2.4 – Right to Petition

Every person in the Unified States shall have the right to petition the government for the redress of grievances. If a petition has verified signatures from at least one percent (1%) of registered voters, the government shall publicly respond to the petition within thirty (30) business days.

5.2.5 – Right to Personal Ideology

No ideology shall be recognized as mandatory by the State or any state.

The State shall guarantee the freedom of political activities not prohibited by the Constitution and the laws of the Unified States.

Section 5.3 – Property Rights

5.3.1 – Right to Bear Arms

Every adult of sound mind has the right to own firearms, provided they are not incarcerated, they have received training on safe use and storage of said firearms and are licensed by the state government.

The firearms in question cannot be fully automatic (fire more than one (1) round per pull of a trigger) or have a magazine capacity of more than thirty (30) rounds. The right to bear arms can be revoked if the person is determined by a court of law to be a danger to themselves or others and/or has been convicted of a violent crime.

5.3.2 – No Soldiers on Private Property

Members of the active Armed Forces may not be allowed to stay in private residences or on private land during peacetime, unless freely authorized in writing by the owner.

5.3.3 – Search and Seizure

No person shall be searched, nor property seized, without specific probable cause.

No one shall be subjected to arbitrary interference with his privacy, family, home or correspondence, nor to attacks upon their honor and reputation.

5.3.4 - Eminent Domain

No person's belongings or property may be seized for public use without at least fair market value compensation.

Public use can never be for the direct benefit of a private business entity or person.

ARTICLE 6 –
OTHER CONSIDERATIONS

Section 6.1 – Federal versus State Legal Scope

6.1.1 – Federal Law Scope

Federal laws shall be enacted which affect the entire State and it would be confusing or impractical for each state to determine their own laws independently. Such laws may include telecommunications, education, healthcare, weapons, and licenses for driving, or piloting an aircraft, boat, or spacecraft.

6.1.2 – States' Powers

All powers not described in this Constitution for the Federal government (State) are reserved for the states.

The people may have other rights not addressed explicitly in this document.

Section 6.2 – Constitutional Amendments

The right to determine and change this Constitution shall belong exclusively to the people and shall not be usurped by the State, its bodies, or officials.

Amendments to this Constitution shall be approved by a simple majority of House and Senate, then presented to the people in the next federal election. A sixty percent (60%) majority of the votes are needed to ratify an Amendment.

Section 6.3 - Citizenship

6.3.1 - Automatic Citizenship

Grandfather clause: Citizens of the *United* States of America at the time of this Constitution's adoption are automatically granted citizenship in the Unified States of America.

Anyone born to parents who are both citizens of the Unified States are automatically citizens, regardless of where they are born.

6.3.2 - Acquired Citizenship

Refugees may be granted two-year (2) temporary citizenship, which will expire when granted permanent resident status or they are removed from the country.

Immigrants are given five (5) years of permanent resident status, after which they should apply for full citizenship or emigrate.

Permanent residents may apply for naturalized citizenship after five (5) years of permanent resident status. They must pass a written or oral test on citizenship duties and Unified States history and swear allegiance to this Constitution.

6.3.3 - Right to Citizenship

Everyone has the right to a nationality, and the right to change that nationality.

Citizens of the Unified States may also have citizenship of up to one (1) other State (dual citizenship), provided the other State does not significantly contradict the rights of the Unified States and allows such dual citizenship.

Section 6.4 - Science and Education

6.4.1 - Science-Based Policies

Laws and policy shall be based on the best evidence-based scientific understanding of the world, while also recognizing that scientific understanding grows over time. Everyone shall take care never to distort scientific facts or statistics to fit one's biases or personal objectives.

Laws and policy shall be based on respect for human rights and the psychological, emotional, spiritual, and philosophical needs of the people.

Federal research areas may include topics that are not deemed financially worthwhile by for-profit institutions. These areas may include, but are not limited to, the effectiveness of naturally occurring plants and fungi (e.g., marijuana, herbs, mushrooms), alternative medicine, and treatment and/or cures for rare diseases or disorders. Research into renewable energy technologies and more efficient paper sources (hemp, bamboo, etc.) should be supported.

Federally funded research should also fuel basic science research needs which may need longer-term commitment and/or more risk than private industry or academia will tolerate.

6.4.2 – Measurement

The International System of Units [REF09] ("SI Units" or "metric system") shall be used for all official business of the State. Other units of historical or traditional relevance may be presented in addition to SI Units, such as "hands" for the height of horses and other *Equidae*, "knots" for marine vessel speed, etc.

The Common Era (CE) and Before Common Era (BCE) Gregorian calendar shall be the default for all government business to avoid the religious bias of AD (Latin *anno domini*, "in the year of the Lord") and BC ("before Christ"). Other calendars can also be referenced when appropriate for clarity, such as Jewish, Chinese, etc.

The start of the federal fiscal year shall be October 1st to avoid conflict with frequent winter holiday celebrations. The start of each fiscal week is Sunday. Working days are considered Monday through Friday, except for Federal holidays.

6.4.3 – Education

Public education shall be provided from kindergarten through 12th grade (K-12) for citizens and residents, including refugees, illegal aliens, and permanent residents.

Meals during public education school hours shall be free of charge.

Funding for public primary and secondary education shall be evenly distributed within an Electoral District based on the number of students in each school and school district.

Parents have the right to choose the kind of education given to their children. Government funding for private or religious education is not permitted.

Public post-secondary education shall be free for two (2) years for all students who qualify and maintain acceptable academic standing. Post-secondary education includes accredited colleges, universities, and trade schools.

Section 6.5 – Campaign Contributions

Donations to political campaigns for State and state elected offices may be made only by individual citizens or residents, subject to a limit of three percent (3%) of the individual's gross income per year per candidate, or $30,000 per candidate, whichever is less. The $30,000 value shall be adjusted annually based on the consumer price index.

Donations may not be made by businesses, non-profit organizations, special interest groups, or corporations.

Section 6.6 – National Census

A National Census shall be taken every twelve (12) years to determine the population characteristics and distribution of citizens and residents in the Unified States.

The results of the National Census shall be made publicly available. They shall be used to determine adjustment of House and Senate representation, school student needs, and other demographic purposes. They may never be used to violate any of the personal, communication, or property rights of the people.

Section 6.7 – Candidate Fitness for Duty

Candidates for the highest Executive, Legislative, and Judicial offices must pass Qualifying Exams, Health Assessments, and Financial Assessments to determine Fitness for Duty. Executive and Legislative candidates must also meet Security Clearance requirements.

6.7.1 – Qualifying Exams

Candidates must demonstrate basic knowledge of State history, government, economic principles, and international relations through oral and/or written examination. This must be completed successfully before assuming office for the first term.

Candidates for a position may be disqualified if they do not pass these exams after no more than two (2) attempts.

6.7.2 – Health Assessments

Candidates must pass tests to assess mental and physical health. Failure to do so will result in disqualification from holding office.

The objective of these tests is to determine if the candidate has any chronic conditions or is taking any medications or supplements which would compromise their ability to perform their duties or protect State interests. Testing must be conducted by providers who have no personal or financial connection to the Candidate, have earned an appropriate terminal degree (such as MD, DO, PsyD, etc.), and a minimum of fifteen (15) years of relevant experience.

Health Assessments must be completed every three (3) years for candidates up to age 50 years, every two years from age 51 to 70, and every year from age 71 on.

6.7.3 – Financial Assessments

Candidates must provide disclosure of personal financial status, including bank records, tax returns, business interests, and worldwide obligations or investments.

Candidates must divest from any personal or business interests which would constitute a conflict of interest or the appearance thereof.

Members of the Executive Branch, Congress and National and State Supreme Court Justices shall have no right to combine their office with other work (except for teaching, research, and creative activities outside of working hours), or to be members of an administrative body or supervisory board (e.g. Board of Directors) of a profit-making enterprise.

Failure to comply with financial assessment shall result in disqualification from holding office, regardless of popular vote or approval of Congress.

6.7.4 – Security Clearances

Members of the Executive and Legislative Branches must qualify for a security clearance using the same procedures as any other State employee. No one under any circumstance shall be given a security clearance automatically. No member of the Executive or Legislative Branches may issue a clearance for any person except Executive personnel who perform and assess such investigations.

Failure to qualify for a needed clearance shall result in disqualification for Executive or Legislative Branch positions, including the President, Vice President, Cabinet positions, Representative, or Senator.

6.7.5 – Applicability and Exemptions

These Assessments apply to the President, Vice President, all Cabinet Secretaries, the Military Master, Department Secretaries, House Representatives, Senators, State Supreme Court Justices, and National Supreme Court Justices.

No one is exempt from Health Assessments per the age-based schedule defined.

No one is exempt from Financial Assessments at the start of each term of service.

National and State Supreme Court Justices are exempt from obtaining a security clearance.

Candidates for the Military Master and Department Secretaries may be exempt from Qualifying Exams if they have at least twenty (20) years of honorable military service as an Officer, ending no more than five (5) years before holding office.

Candidates for the State and National Supreme Court Justices may be exempt from Qualifying Exams if they have earned a *Juris Doctor* (J.D.) degree and have served honorably as a judge for a minimum of fifteen (15) years, ending no more than five years before holding office.

Section 6.8 – Official Language

The Unified States do not have an Official Language. American English is the default language for government communications.

Electoral Districts may define Official Language(s) in addition to American English to meet the needs of their population.

Section 6.9 – Taxation

Everyone shall pay taxes and duties in the manner and to the extent established by law.

Section 6.10 – Budgetary System

The budgetary system of the Unified States shall be based on the principles of fair and impartial distribution of social wealth among citizens and territorial communities.

Section 6.11 – Territory Status

Territories may be added to the Unified States in accordance with international treaties.

Territories with a permanent human population must change status after no more than twenty-four (24) years. They may apply to Congress to become states, become independent, or associate with another State.

The will of the people in the territory should be the deciding factor in its desired change of status.

Congress may approve statehood by a simple majority in both House and Senate.

Section 6.12 – Definitions

The terms "shall" or "will" are used in the requirements document sense to indicate a mandatory thing. "Should" means highly recommended but not absolute. "May" or "might" means optional or as needed.

The author uses "black" to denote people with more recent African heritage instead of "African American," because the latter indicates American nationality which isn't necessarily true or relevant. People who are not white are collectively called "people of color."

"Adult" is defined as a person reaching the age of majority, typically eighteen (18) years, but also including minors who have declared emancipation from their parents. "Adult" excludes those who are not mentally competent, such as due to severe mental illness or catastrophic injury.

There are several categories of people referenced in this Constitution.

- "Visitors" are people who do not reside in the Unified States but are present for a brief period of time for personal and/or business reasons.

- "Residents" are people who live in the Unified States indefinitely but are not citizens. They may include permanent residents, refugees, immigrants, and illegal aliens.

- Homeless people could be residents or citizens.

- "Citizens" are people who live in the Unified States or abroad and are citizens by birth or naturalization. Only citizens may vote and serve in government positions above the local level.

- "The people" and "Everyone" and "All people" includes visitors, residents, and citizens.

- "Incarcerated people" are people who have been convicted of serious criminal violations. Incarcerated people reside in a jail or prison, and may be citizens, residents, or visitors.

Measurement and calendar definitions are described under section 6.4.2.

REFERENCES

01 | https://constitutioncenter.org/media/files/constitution.pdf

02 | https://ihl-databases.icrc.org/assets/treaties/380-GC-IV-EN.pdf

Collective punishment is also prohibited by the Geneva Convention of 1949, Article 33.

03 | https://thesatanictemple.com/blogs/the-satanic-temple-tenets/there-are-seven-fundamental-tenets

04 | https://hcj.gov.ua/sites/default/files/field/file/the_constitution_of_ukraine.pdf

05 | https://www.archives.gov/files/press/press-kits/magna-carta/magna-carta-translation.pdf

06 | https://www.constituteproject.org/constitution/Norway_2014.pdf

07 | https://www.engageny.org/file/2191/download/the_constitution_of_the_iroquois_nations.pdf

08 | https://www.gp.org/ten_key_values

09 | https://www.nist.gov/pml/owm/metric-si/si-units

10 | https://www.un.org/en/udhrbook/pdf/udhr_booklet_en_web.pdf

11 | https://www.un.org/Depts/los/convention_agreements/convention_overview_convention.htm

12 | https://en.wikipedia.org/wiki/K%C3%A1rm%C3%A1n_line

APPENDIX A.
MAPPING TO
SOURCE DOCUMENTS

Table A-1 shows which Constitution sections are inspired by each of these sources. The purpose of this mapping is to show that many of the rights and principles in this Constitution are drawn from a range of historic cultures. The sources are:

- The United States **Constitution** through Amendment 27 (XXVII). For example, A14.1 means Amendment 14, section 1.

- The Constitution of **Ukraine** as of April 26, 2023

- **Green** Party Ten Key Values (Appendix D)

- **Iroquois** Constitution

- **Norway**'s Constitution of 1814

- Seven Tenets of the Satanic **Temple** (Appendix C)

- The United Nations' Universal Declaration of **Human Rights** (Appendix B)

- The **Magna Carta** (NARA translation), 1215 CE

Section	Constitution	Ukraine	Green	Iroquois	Norway	Temple	Human Rights	Magna Carta
PREAMBLE	Preamble							
ARTICLE 0 – FOUNDING PRINCIPLES								
Section 0.1 – Life	A14.1	3, 21, 27, 68	2			4	01, 03, 29	
Section 0.2 – Fallibility						6		
Section 0.3 – Personal Dignity and Actualization		15, 23, 28, 54	9		100		22, 27	
Section 0.4 - Government Purpose								
Section 0.5 - Legislative Purpose		55			19			
Section 0.6 - Punishment Authority								
Section 0.7 - Role in Nature		13, 14	3, 10		112	1		
ARTICLE 1 – INTRODUCTION								
Section 1.1 – Inspiration for this Constitution								
Section 1.2 – Branches of Government		6, 19		5				17

Section								
Section 1.3 – Type of Government	4.4	1, 2, 5	1	93			21	30
Section 1.4 – Type of Economy		42	5				17	
Section 1.5 – International Relations Goals		9, 18	9		115			
Section 1.6 – Property Ownership							17	
Section 1.7 – Duties of the People			4				21	
ARTICLE 2 – EXECUTIVE BRANCH								
Section 2.1 – Office of the President	2.1	102						
2.1.1 – Define President's Cabinet		113						
2.1.2 – President Qualifications	2.1	103						
2.1.3 – President Election and Term of Office	A22.1							
2.1.4 – Removal of President	1.3, 2.4	108, 111						
2.1.5 – President Responsibilities and Powers	2.2, 2.3	106			20, 21, 25			
Section 2.2 – Office of the Vice President								

Appendix A

Section	Constitution	Ukraine	Green	Iroquois	Norway	Temple	Human Rights	Magna Carta
2.2.1 – Vice President Qualifications								
2.2.2 – Vice President Election and Term								
2.2.3 – Removal of Vice President								
2.2.4 – Vice President Responsibilities and Powers								
Section 2.3 – Office of the Armed Forces		17, 107						
2.3.1 – Define Military Master								
2.3.2 – Armed Forces Departments								
2.3.3 – Define Department Secretaries								
2.3.4 – Required Military Service		65		37, 81	26, 119			
2.3.5 – Veterans' Affairs		17						
Section 2.4 – Line of Succession	A20.3, A25	112						
ARTICLE 3 – LEGISLATIVE BRANCH	1.1	6, 75		9				

Appendix A

50

Section 3.1 – The House of Representatives					
3.1.1 – House Purpose	1.5, 1.7, 1.8			57	
3.1.2 – Electoral Districts Scope		132			
3.1.3 – Electoral District Boundaries Defined					
3.1.4 – Representative Qualifications	1.2, A14.3		21		
3.1.5 – Representative Term	1.2				
3.1.6 – House Chief Representative Defined			14		
Section 3.2 – The Senate					
3.2.1 – Senate Purpose	1.3	94			
3.2.2 – Number of Senators	A17				
3.2.3 – Senator Qualifications	1.3, A14.3, A17		35		
3.2.4 – Senator Term	1.3				
3.2.5 – Chief Senator Defined					

Section	Constitution	Ukraine	Green	Iroquois	Norway	Temple	Human Rights	Magna Carta
Section 3.3 – Congress Impeachment					86			
ARTICLE 4 – JUDICIAL BRANCH		6, 124						
Section 4.1 – National Supreme Court	3.1, 3.2	125, 147						
4.1.1 – National Supreme Court Justice Qualifications		127			91			
4.1.2 – National Supreme Court Justice Term								
4.1.3 – National Supreme Court Justice Selection		128						
Section 4.2 – State Supreme Courts	3.1							
4.2.1 – State Supreme Court Justice Qualifications		127						
4.2.2 – State Supreme Court Justice Term								
4.2.3 – State Supreme Court Justice Selection								

Appendix A

Principle							
Section 4.3 – Core Legal Principles							
4.3.1 – Rule of Law		8, 19, 57, 68					
4.3.2 – Personhood							06
4.3.3 – Voting Rights	A14.2, A15.1, A19, A24.1, A26	38, 69-71			49, 50, 53		
4.3.4 – Immunity from Prosecution	A11	60, 105					
4.3.5 – Martial Law		64					
4.3.6 – Treason Defined	3.3	111		25	85		30
4.3.7 – Air and Sea Boundaries							
4.3.8 – Single State							
Section 4.4 – Pretrial Rights							
4.4.1 – No Arbitrary Arrest or Custody	A14.1	29			113		09
4.4.2 – Presumption of Innocence		62			96		11

Appendix A

53

Section	Constitution	Ukraine	Green	Iroquois	Norway	Temple	Human Rights	Magna Carta
4.4.3 – No Self Incrimination	A5	63						
4.4.4 – Right to Representation		59						
4.4.5 – Proportional Bail	A8							14
Section 4.5 – Trial Rights								
4.5.1 – Right to Trial	1.9, A5, A7, A14.1	29, 58			94, 97		10, 11	29
4.5.2 – No Double Jeopardy	A5	61						
4.5.3 – Judicial Decisions		129				2, 7		
4.5.4 – Speedy Trial	A6	29			95			
4.5.5 – Right to Appeal							08	26
Section 4.6 – Punishment Rights								
4.6.1 – No Collective or Kin Punishment [REF02]		61						
4.6.2 – No Capital Punishment or Torture		28		20	93			

Section 4.7 – Recusal of Justices		126						
Section 4.8 – Impeachment of Justices								
ARTICLE 5 – BILL OF RIGHTS								
Section 5.1 – Personal Rights								
5.1.1 – Equal Rights Statement	A15, A19	21, 24	7, 8				02	
5.1.2 – Survival Rights		47, 48			104		25	
5.1.3 – Right to Healthcare		24, 49					25	
5.1.4 – Right to Bodily Autonomy						3		
5.1.5 – Freedom from Religion	6, A1	35		99	16		18	63
5.1.6 – Equal Protection	A14				98		07	
5.1.7 – Personal Movement		33		71	106		13, 14	42
5.1.8 – Marriage		51		43			16	6
5.1.9 – Worker's Rights		36, 43-45	6		101, 110		23, 24	

Appendix A

55

Section	Constitution	Ukraine	Green	Iroquois	Norway	Temple	Human Rights	Magna Carta
5.1.10 – No Slavery	A13						04, 05	
5.1.11 – Right to Heritage		11, 66		99	108			9
5.1.12 – Consumer Protection		42						
5.1.13 – Environmental Protection		13, 14, 16, 50	10		112			
5.1.14 – Parenthood Rights		52						
5.1.15 – Children's Work Rights								
Section 5.2 – Communication Rights								
5.2.1 – Free Speech	A1	15, 34			100		19	
5.2.2 – Freedom of Media	A1	31					19	
5.2.3 – Right to Assembly and Association	A1	36-39, 57	1		101		20	
5.2.4 – Right to Petition	A1	40						
5.2.5 – Right to Personal Ideology		15, 34						

Appendix A

Section							
Section 5.3 – Property Rights							
5.3.1 – Right to Bear Arms	A2						
5.3.2 – No Soldiers on Private Property	A3						
5.3.3 – Search and Seizure	A4	30, 32, 41		102		12	8
5.3.4 - Eminent Domain	A5	41		105			21
ARTICLE 6 – OTHER CONSIDERATIONS							
Section 6.1 – Federal versus State Legal Scope							
6.1.1 – Federal Law Scope	A9	22					
6.1.2 – States' Powers	A10						
Section 6.2 – Constitutional Amendments	5	154-157	16	121			
Section 6.3 – Citizenship		4, 25					
6.3.1 – Automatic Citizenship	A14.1						
6.3.2 – Acquired Citizenship	A14.1		68, 75				

Section	Constitution	Ukraine	Green	Iroquois	Norway	Temple	Human Rights	Magna Carta
6.3.3 – Right to Citizenship	A14.1						15	
Section 6.4 – Science and Education								
6.4.1 – Science-based Policies						5		
6.4.2 – Measurement								25
6.4.3 – Education		53			109		26	
Section 6.5 – Campaign Contributions								
Section 6.6 – National Census								
Section 6.7 – Candidate Fitness for Duty								
6.7.1 – Qualifying Exams								
6.7.2 – Health Assessments		110		21				
6.7.3 – Financial Assessments		120						
6.7.4 – Security Clearances								

Appendix A

6.7.5 – Applicability and Exemptions					
Section 6.8 – Official Language	1.8, A16	10			
Section 6.9 – Taxation		67	18		
Section 6.10 – Budgetary System		95-98			
Section 6.11 –Territory Status					
Section 6.12 – Definitions					

Appendix A

59

APPENDIX B.
THE UNITED NATIONS'
UNIVERSAL DECLARATION OF
HUMAN RIGHTS

01

All human beings are born free and equal in dignity and rights. They are endowed with reason and conscience and should act towards one another in a spirit of brotherhood.

02

Everyone is entitled to all the rights and freedoms set forth in this Declaration, without distinction of any kind, such as race, colour, sex, language, religion, political or other opinion, national or social origin, property, birth or other status. Furthermore, no distinction shall be made on the basis of the political, jurisdictional or international status of the country or territory to which a person belongs, whether it be independent, trust, non-self-governing or under any other limitation of sovereignty.

03

Everyone has the right to life, liberty and security of person.

04

No one shall be held in slavery or servitude; slavery and the slave trade shall be prohibited in all their forms.

05

No one shall be subjected to torture or to cruel, inhuman or degrading treatment or punishment.

06

Everyone has the right to recognition everywhere as a person before the law.

07

All are equal before the law and are entitled without any discrimination to equal protection of the law. All are entitled to equal protection against any discrimination in violation of this Declaration and against any incitement to such discrimination.

08

Everyone has the right to an effective remedy by the competent national tribunals for acts violating the fundamental rights granted him by the constitution or by law.

09

No one shall be subjected to arbitrary arrest, detention or exile.

10

Everyone is entitled in full equality to a fair and public hearing by an independent and impartial tribunal, in the determination of his rights and obligations and of any criminal charge against him.

11

(1) Everyone charged with a penal offence has the right to be presumed innocent until proved guilty according to law in a public trial at which he has had all the guarantees necessary for his defence.

(2) No one shall be held guilty of any penal offence on account of any act or omission which did not constitute a penal offence, under national or international law, at the time when it was committed. Nor shall a heavier penalty be imposed than the one that was applicable at the time the penal offence was committed.

12

No one shall be subjected to arbitrary interference with his privacy, family, home or correspondence, nor to attacks upon his honour and reputation. Everyone has the right to the protection of the law against such interference or attacks.

13

(1) Everyone has the right to freedom of movement and residence within the borders of each State.

(2) Everyone has the right to leave any country, including his own, and to return to his country.

14

(1) Everyone has the right to seek and to enjoy in other countries asylum from persecution.

(2) This right may not be invoked in the case of prosecutions genuinely arising from non-political crimes or from acts contrary to the purposes and principles of the United Nations.

15

(1) Everyone has the right to a nationality.

(2) No one shall be arbitrarily deprived of his nationality nor denied the right to change his nationality.

16

(1) Men and women of full age, without any limitation due to race, nationality or religion, have the right to marry and to found a family. They are entitled to equal rights as to marriage, during marriage and at its dissolution.

(2) Marriage shall be entered into only with the free and full consent of the intending spouses.

(3) The family is the natural and fundamental group unit of society and is entitled to protection by society and the State

17

(1) Everyone has the right to own property alone as well as in association with others.

(2) No one shall be arbitrarily deprived of his property.

18

Everyone has the right to freedom of thought, conscience and religion; this right includes freedom to change his religion or belief, and freedom, either alone or in community with others and in public or private, to manifest his religion or belief in teaching, practice, worship and observance.

19

Everyone has the right to freedom of opinion and expression; this right includes freedom to hold opinions without interference and to seek, receive and impart information and ideas through any media and regardless of frontiers.

20

(1) Everyone has the right to freedom of peaceful assembly and association.

(2) No one may be compelled to belong to an association

21

(1) Everyone has the right to take part in the government of his country, directly or through freely chosen representatives.

(2) Everyone has the right to equal access to public service in his country.

(3) The will of the people shall be the basis of the authority of government; this will shall be expressed in periodic and genuine

elections which shall be by universal and equal suffrage and shall be held by secret vote or by equivalent free voting procedures.

22

Everyone, as a member of society, has the right to social security and is entitled to realization, through national effort and international cooperation and in accordance with the organization and resources of each State, of the economic, social and cultural rights indispensable for his dignity and the free development of his personality.

23

(1) Everyone has the right to work, to free choice of employment, to just and favourable conditions of work and to protection against unemployment.

(2) Everyone, without any discrimination, has the right to equal pay for equal work.

(3) Everyone who works has the right to just and favourable remuneration ensuring for himself and his family an existence worthy of human dignity, and supplemented, if necessary, by other means of social protection.

(4) Everyone has the right to form and to join trade unions for the protection of his interests

24

Everyone has the right to rest and leisure, including reasonable limitation of working hours and periodic holidays with pay.

25

(1) Everyone has the right to a standard of living adequate for the health and well-being of himself and of his family, including food, clothing, housing and medical care and necessary social services, and the right to security in the event of unemployment, sickness, disability, widowhood, old age or other lack of livelihood in circumstances beyond his control.

(2) Motherhood and childhood are entitled to special care and assistance. All children, whether born in or out of wedlock, shall enjoy the same social protection.

26

(1) Everyone has the right to education. Education shall be free, at least in the elementary and fundamental stages. Elementary education shall be compulsory. Technical and professional education shall be made generally available and higher education shall be equally accessible to all on the basis of merit.

(2) Education shall be directed to the full development of the human personality and to the strengthening of respect for human rights and fundamental freedoms. It shall promote understanding, tolerance and friendship among all nations, racial or religious groups, and shall further the activities of the United Nations for the maintenance of peace.

(3) Parents have a prior right to choose the kind of education that shall be given to their children.

27

(1) Everyone has the right freely to participate in the cultural life of the community, to enjoy the arts and to share in scientific advancement and its benefits.

(2) Everyone has the right to the protection of the moral and material interests resulting from any scientific, literary or artistic production of which he is the author.

28

Everyone is entitled to a social and international order in which the rights and freedoms set forth in this Declaration can be fully realized.

29

(1) Everyone has duties to the community in which alone the free and full development of his personality is possible.

(2) In the exercise of his rights and freedoms, everyone shall be subject only to such limitations as are determined by law solely for the purpose of securing due recognition and respect for the rights and freedoms of others and of meeting the just requirements of morality, public order and the general welfare in a democratic society.

(3) These rights and freedoms may in no case be exercised contrary to the purposes and principles of the United Nations.

30

Nothing in this Declaration may be interpreted as implying for any State, group or person any right to engage in any activity or to perform any act aimed at the destruction of any of the rights and freedoms set forth herein.

From [REF10].

APPENDIX C.
THE SEVEN FUNDAMENTAL
TENETS OF THE SATANIC TEMPLE

I

One should strive to act with compassion and empathy toward all creatures in accordance with reason.

II

The struggle for justice is an ongoing and necessary pursuit that should prevail over laws and institutions.

III

One's body is inviolable, subject to one's own will alone.

IV

The freedoms of others should be respected, including the freedom to offend. To willfully and unjustly encroach upon the freedoms of another is to forgo one's own.

V

Beliefs should conform to one's best scientific understanding of the world. One should take care never to distort scientific facts to fit one's beliefs.

VI

People are fallible. If one makes a mistake, one should do one's best to rectify it and resolve any harm that might have been caused.

VII

Every tenet is a guiding principle designed to inspire nobility in action and thought. The spirit of compassion, wisdom, and justice should always prevail over the written or spoken word.

From [REF03].

APPENDIX D.
GREEN PARTY TEN KEY VALUES

1. Grassroots Democracy

All human beings must be allowed a say in decisions that affect their lives; no one should be subject to the will of another. We work to improve public participation in every aspect of government and seek to ensure that our public representatives are fully accountable to the people who elect them. We also work to create new types of political organizations that expand the process of participatory democracy by directly including citizens in decision-making.

2. Social Justice and Equal Opportunity

As a matter of right, all persons must have the opportunity to benefit equally from the resources afforded us by society and the environment. We must consciously confront in ourselves, our organizations, and society at large, any discrimination by race, class, gender, sexual orientation, age, nationality, religion, or physical or mental ability that denies fair treatment and equal justice under the law.

3. Ecological Wisdom

Human societies must function with the understanding that we are part of nature, not separate from nature. We must maintain an ecological balance and live within the ecological and resource limits of our communities and our planet. We support a sustainable society that utilizes resources in such a way that future generations will benefit and not suffer from the practices of our generation.

To this end we must practice agriculture that replenishes the soil, move to an energy-efficient economy, and live in ways that respect the integrity of natural systems.

4. Non-Violence

It is essential that we develop effective alternatives to society's current patterns of violence. We will work to demilitarize and eliminate weapons of mass destruction, without being naive about the intentions of other governments. We recognize the need for self-defense and the defense of others who are in danger. We promote non-violent methods to oppose practices and policies with which we disagree, and will guide our actions toward lasting personal, community and global peace.

5. Decentralization

Centralization of wealth and power contributes to social and economic injustice, environmental destruction, and militarization. We seek a restructuring of social, political and economic institutions away from a system controlled by and mostly benefiting the powerful few, to a democratic, less bureaucratic system. Decision-making should, as much as possible, remain at the individual and local level, while assuring that civil rights are protected for all.

6. Community-Based Economics

We support redesigning our work structures to encourage employee ownership and workplace democracy. We support developing new economic activities and institutions that allow us to use technology in ways that are humane, freeing, ecological, and responsive and accountable to communities. We support establishing a form of basic economic security open to all. We call for moving beyond the narrow 'job ethic' to new definitions of 'work,' 'jobs' and 'income' in a cooperative and democratic economy. We support restructuring our patterns of income distribution to reflect the wealth created by those outside the formal monetary economy – those who take responsibility for parenting, housekeeping, home gardens, community volunteer work, and the like. We support restricting the size and concentrated power of corporations without discouraging superior efficiency or technological innovation.

7. Feminism and Gender Equity

We have inherited a social system based on male domination of politics and economics. We call for the replacement of the cultural ethics of domination and control with cooperative ways of interacting that respect differences of opinion and gender. Human values such as gender equity, interpersonal responsibility, and honesty must be developed with moral conscience. We recognize that the processes for determining our decisions and actions are just as important as achieving the outcomes we want.

8. Respect for Diversity

We believe it is important to value cultural, ethnic, racial, sexual, religious and spiritual diversity, and to promote the development of respectful relationships across the human spectrum. We believe that the many diverse elements of society should be reflected in our organizations and decision-making bodies, and we support the leadership of people who have been traditionally closed out of leadership roles. We encourage respect for all life forms, and increased attention to the preservation of biodiversity.

9. Personal and Global Responsibility

We encourage individuals to act to improve their personal wellbeing and, at the same time, to enhance ecological balance and social harmony. We seek to join with people and organizations around the world to foster peace, economic justice, and the health of the planet.

10. Future Focus and Sustainability

Our actions and policies should be motivated by long-term goals. We seek to protect valuable natural resources, safely disposing of or 'unmaking' all waste we create, while developing a sustainable economics that does not depend on continual expansion for survival. We must counterbalance the drive for short-term profits by assuring that economic development, new technologies, and fiscal policies are responsible to future generations who will inherit the results of our actions. We must make the quality of all lives, rather than open-ended economic growth, the focus of future thinking and policy.

From [REF08].

About the Author

Jennifer M. Booker, BS, MS, Ph.D., BSN, RN, is not a lawyer. She regards this as a bonus for rewriting the Constitution so it can be better understood by people who are also not lawyers.

She has earned three engineering degrees (BS, MS, Ph.D.), worked extensively in the defense and aviation industries, was a professor of computing for two decades, and earned a nursing degree (BSN) and Registered Nurse license. In addition, she has done extensive studies of social sciences, including political science, psychology, and gender studies. Her website is jenbooker.com.

This is Dr. Booker's second book. Her first book was *The New Normal: Coming out as Transgender in Midlife* (2019), also from The Unbound Press.

jenbooker.com